NOTES ON THE BOOK OF REVELATION

Harvesting Through the Scriptures

Isiah King Sr., MMin

ISBN 978-1-63961-452-3 (paperback)
ISBN 978-1-63961-453-0 (digital)

Copyright © 2021 by Isiah King Sr., MMin

All rights reserved. No part of this publication may be reproduced, distributed, or transmitted in any form or by any means, including photocopying, recording, or other electronic or mechanical methods without the prior written permission of the publisher. For permission requests, solicit the publisher via the address below.

Christian Faith Publishing, Inc.
832 Park Avenue
Meadville, PA 16335
www.christianfaithpublishing.com

Printed in the United States of America

DEDICATION

This book is dedicated to my loving wife, who has been by my side and has helped me in what God has given me to do. She has been my encourager. To my deceased parents, who taught me about the Lord and were examples of how Christians should live.

CHAPTER 1

1:1-3

The introductory words to this opening paragraph let us know the content matter of this prophetic book. It begins by saying the Revelation of Jesus Christ. The Greek word for our English word *revelation* is the word ἀποκάλυψις /*apokalypsis,* and it means "an unveiling" or "a disclosure."

From the Greek word ἀποκάλυψις /*apokalypsis* we get our English word *apocalypse*, which means "to uncover." Therefore, the book of Revelation is about future events that are uncovered or revealed by Jesus Christ, which were told to Him by God the Father.

Christ in turn tells his angel to inform this heavenly message to John, the beloved disciple; John then tells the servants about things that must soon take place. Let me also add that this word *servant* would include the seven Churches of Asia, as well as all those who follow him and have a relationship with Christ today.

The uncovered events that must soon take place are referring to an immediate point of time in the prophetic future where these events will start happening quickly and in succession. The Greek word τάχος/ *Taxoc* translates to our English words *shortly, soon, quickness*, and *speedily*. Let me also add that even though these future events have not happened yet, let us not get to comfortable with its delay, because when it does happen, it will be likened to an unexpected storm that ruins and interrupts eveyone's plans of daily living. When these events occur, the people will be shocked and surprised. Why? Because they will not be looking for it to happen. It's going to happen suddenly and quickly. It's going to happen so quick that people won't believe what they see or hear. That's why John the revelator said in verse 3, "Blessed is he that readeth and they that hear the words of this prophecy, and keep those things which are written therein: for the time is at hand." In other words, this prophetic book was written to unveil and prepare mankind to get their hearts right with Christ because these future events will take place, and there will be nothing that mankind can do to stop it. These unveilings were given to John, the beloved the disciple, who is identified in this first verse as his servant as well.

Notice the word *servant* as it applies to John: it is the Greek word δοῦλος /*doulos,* which means slave or bondslave, or one who is in subjection to another. This word gives us a picture of the close and subservient relationship that John had with our Lord Christ. It was the spiritual mindset of John to do his master's will; his will, as well as his self desires, didn't matter. To serve Christ and to bring about his spiritual objectives was all that mattered to John. He sought to do the master's will, and he did it with such love, commitment, and unwavering passion. Christ knew that John had much love for him, and with that love came undying trust. Matter of fact, the love and trust that John demonstrated to Christ was such an exemplification of loyalty that Christ left the care of his mother in John's hands when he was being crucified on the cross. Christ said on the cross, "Woman, behold thy son! Then saith he to the disciple, Behold thy mother! And from that hour that disciple took her unto his own home" (John 19:26).

John was also an apostle and eyewitness of Jesus Christ and wrote of all the things that the angel had heard of Jesus. Also, it appears in verse 3, when a believer reads and hears with understanding the message that this book of prophecy is trying to convey, that God will add a blessing to their life.

1:4–8

John in his salutation lets us know who the recipients of this book are, as well as its destination. He addresses the book to the seven churches that are in the Roman province of Asia Minor. But before we continue, let's define the word *Church*. In Greek, it's the word εκκλησια/*ekklesia* and it means "to be called out." This definition reminds believers of their spiritual journey and purpose in Christ, for Christ has called his people from the world of sin into a life of light and salvation. Again, these Churches were in the Roman province of Asia. This is to say that this area or district was under the governmental authority of the Roman Empire.

Even though there were more than seven churches located in province on Asia Minor such as Colossae, (Col 1:2), Hierapolis (Col 4:13), Troas (2 Cor 2:12, Acts 20:5), Miletus (Acts 20:17), Magnesia, and Tralles. John only mentioned the following churches, which are Ephesus, Smyrna, Pergamum, Thyatira, Sardis, Philadelphia, and Laodicea. This could be because of the mail districts where the churches were located.

Also, in John's greetings to the seven churches are the words *Grace* and *Peace*. These words assure the believer that spiritual blessings are bestowed upon all who are in right standing with God.

The word *grace* in Greek is the word χαρις/*charis* and it means *favor, pleasure, joy, kindness* and *gift*. The word *peace* in Greek is the word ειρηνη/*eirene*, which means "freedom from worry," "safety," and "prosperity." It also means "to be free from rage and havoc." Therefore, John the revelator wishes and prays for God's grace and peace to be upon those churches in Asia.

It must be noted that as God's Church strives down the road of spiritual maturity, as it journeys through the halls of sanctification and unity, let us be mindful that every spiritual virtue and gift come by way of growing and maturing in Christ.

John, the beloved, lets us know that the source of all blessings, the source of all peace, and the source of all prosperity comes by Jesus Christ and from the fullness of the Holy Spirit (Jas 1:17; Phil 4:17). John declared that these divine blessings come from God, who is described as being the one *who is*, and *who was*, and *who is to come* (1:8). These words describe God as being eternal and immutable.

God is eternal because he has no beginning or end. The Psalmist said, "Before the mountains were brought forth, or ever thou hadst formed the earth and the world, even from everlasting, thou art God"

(Psalm 90:2). Elihu speaks of God eternal attribute by saying, "the number of his years is unsearchable" (Job 36:26). *Who is* and *who was* also speaks about God never changing over time. He is immutable; He does not change. The writer of Hebrews states, "Jesus Christ is the same yesterday and today and forever" (Heb 13:8).

As we further investigate verse 4, we see that Christ gives divine blessings, favor, and prosperity to the seven Churches of Asia Minor and lets them know that they have no need to worry about their present life circumstance because they have been set free and empowered by the seven spirits of God, which is the Holy Spirit. As we look at verse 4, we see that the number seven has spiritual and historical significance. It is to show fullness and completion.

In Genesis 1:31; 2:–3, God created the heavens and the earth in six days, but on the seventh day he rested from all his work. This is to say that God chose the seventh day to rest and to show that his work was fully completed. Let me also add that when God rested, that does not mean that God is a God that needs to rest or that he is a God that weakens, but it is to say that he chose to stop on that particular day.

It is also to show that mankind needs to take a rest from all his labors and focus his attention on God.

We serve a God that neither slumbers nor sleeps (Psalm 121:4). The number seven was also used when it came to sin offerings; the priest would dip his finger in the blood of the sacrificed bullock and then sprinkle the blood seven times before the lord in front of the temple veil (Lev. 4:16–18).

Then when it came down to God disciplining Israel, he uses the number seven as well (Lev. 26:18–28). Notice that these seven spirits are before the throne of God. This could mean that the Holy Spirit is allowing himself to be willing and accessible to the command of God.

We draw this conclusion from Revelation 7:14, which states, "Therefore are they before the throne of God, and serve him day and night in his temple: and he that sitteth on the throne shall dwell among them." We also see reference of the Trinity in verses 4 and 5. God the Father is mentioned with the word, which is, and which was, and *which is to come*.

The Holy Spirit is described as the seven spirits before his throne, and in verse 5 Christ is mentioned as *who is the faithful witness and the first begotten of the dead*. The Greek word for *faithful* is the word πιστος/*pistos*. It describes Christ as being trusty, true, worthy, loyal, steadfast, and believing. The Greek word for *witness* is the word μαρτυς/*martus*, which translates into our English word *martyr*.

When Christ reigned on earth as 100 percent man, he proved himself to be true to his Father in heaven and to his ministry on earth. He bore witness and testified on those things that he heard his Father say. Jesus said in John 8:26–27, "I have many things to say and to judge of you: but he that sent me is true; and I speak to the world those things which I have heard of him. They understood not that he spoke to them of the Father." Christ also was a martyr. His religious conviction was so dear and true to him that he was willing to die for his cause and mission. He was obedient to the will of his Father all the way to the cross. The apostle Paul said, "And being found in fashion as a man, he humbled himself, and became obedient unto death, even the death of the cross" (Phil 2:8).

Also, in verse 5, Christ is known as the first begotten of the dead, as well as the prince of kings from the earth. I will try to explain and define both interpretations.

First, Jesus is known as the first begotten; the Greek word for first begotten is the word, πρωτοτοκος/*prototokos* and it means that which pertains to be a firstborn child. It was also used to describe a family's oldest son. The nation of Israel is called by God and his son (Gen. 22:21).

Christ is called the first begotten from the dead because he was the only man in history that died and was totally resurrected back to life in a glorified body.

Since the conception of the earth, millions of people died, but there was only one who came back from the dead and remains alive, and his name is Jesus. Yes, friends, Jesus conquered death. The apostle Paul said, "But now is Christ risen from the dead, and become the first fruits of them that slept" (1 Cor 15:20).

Christ is then called the prince of the kings of the earth. This title "The prince of the kings of earth" describes Christ's position during the millennium reign. God the Father will give him a highly exalted name, and people will have to confess that Jesus is the Christ.

The apostle Paul says, "Wherefore God also hath highly exalted him, and given him a name which is above every name: That at the name of Jesus every knee should bow, of things in heaven and things in earth, and things under the earth; And that every tongue should confess that Jesus Christ is Lord, to the glory of God the Father" (Phil 2:9–11). We also learn in verse 5 that God loves his people and that he writes briefly about his redemptive plan of salvation (Isa. 53:1–6, John 3:16, 1 Peter 1:18–19, Eph 2:13, 1 John 1:7).

As we go into verse 6, John says the believers are and have been made kings and priests unto God.

For a reference of what Christians are to be called, one can read Exodus 19:6 and 1 Peter 2:9. What a recommendation! What an honor to be called such a great name by God! We as believers will have a royal and priestly title that denotes spiritual maturity and honors and in sharing the teachings of heavenly principles. What a great position to be in, and that is to teach beside and with the master of all teachers—Christ!

When we take a good look at verse 7, it describes the physical coming of our Lord and Savior Jesus Christ to earth. This is not the Rapture that the apostle Paul writes about in 1 Thessalonians 4th chapter, starting at the 13–18 verse. Simply because when Christ appears during the Rapture he will not touch or descend to earth. Believers in Christ will meet him in the air.

This scripture is about the second coming of Christ when he will come and descend to earth when he will began reigning as king and when he will establish his kingdom. When Christ returns, those who were against him will begin to cry in anguish because they will have no place with Him. In other words, the world or better yet, unbelievers, will not want to see him because condemnation awaits them at his coming (Rev. 21:8).

As we begin to examine verse 8, John lets us know that Christ is eternal. He was in the beginning, and he will definitely be around in eternity. To give us clearer understanding, let's look at the Greek letters alpha and omega in the Greek alphabet. Alpha is the first letter of the Greek alphabet, and omega is the last.

This is to mean that Christ was there in the beginning, and he will be there in eternity. In other words, Christ is and will ever be in existence. He is the God of eternity that has a mandate to come to conquer evil and establish his kingdom. He is the Almighty God. He is strong. John the beloved disciple said, "And out of his mouth goeth a sharp sword, that with it he should smite the nations: and he shall rule them with a rod of iron: and he treadeth the winepress of the fierceness and wrath of Almighty God" (Rev. 19:15).

1:9–17

As we approach verses 9–11, the apostle John tells us of his mission, as well as his location. John tells us first of all that we share in kinship relationship with him; he says that he is our brother. Not by way of being a brother biologically, but being a brother by sharing in the same faith and ministry of Jesus Christ.

When John used the words "Your brother, and companion in tribulation," he was referring to his present trouble under the Roman emperor Domitian. It was Domitian who sentenced him to the deserted isle of Patmos for evangelizing and propagating the Kingdom of God. To show the hardship and dehumanization of John's imprisonment, the isle of Patmos was a rocky, barren, and desolate place where the Roman Government sentenced criminals to carry out their sentences of hard labor by working in the Patmos mines. It was here where John was numbered and placed in the same situation as the malefactors. It is said that when the Roman Emperor couldn't kill John by boiling him in oil that he decided to exile him to Patmos. He did this because by John enduring the boiling oil and coming out unscathed, it only brought more attention to the Gospel that he so passionately preached. However, after Domitian died, he was set free and died a natural death in Ephesus during the reign of Trajan in AD 100. He was born in AD 6. As a side note, John the Revelator was the youngest of the apostles and the last of the twelve apostles that died. In other words, he was exiled on the isle of Patmos for preaching the gospel of Jesus Christ.

The tribulation that John was referring to was not the Great Tribulation of seven years that will take place after the Church will be Raptured from the earth, but it was the persecution that was happening to the first-century Church during John's time; this would be sometime during AD 96. John was exiled on the isle of Patmos for ten years, from AD 86 to AD 96.

Think about it, friends. John spent ten years of quality time with Christ. The Roman emperor didn't know that he was sentencing John, the beloved disciple, to ten years of devotion with God. How much time are we spending with God? Spending quality time with God gives believers countless insights into the treasures of heaven. Notice the insights of what John saw and heard. First of all, because John was spending genuine and quality time with Christ, that divine connection allowed him to be in a spiritual realm with Christ. He said that he was in the Spirit on the Lord's Day.

This is to say that the Holy Spirit enlightened John while he was on the isle of Patmos about things that are in heaven and things that were going to take place on earth. The Holy Spirit opened the doors of heaven, so John can see and hear for himself those things that must shortly come to pass. The Holy Spirit is the only vehicle that can transport man into the environment of the supernatural presence of God, while never moving the physical body from its present location.

John then makes reference to the "Lord's Day." What is the Lord's Day? Some say that this is a reference to the Great Tribulation period where God is going to pronounce judgment on the earth for seven years. However, I feel that the reference to the Day of the Lord is when attention is given to God for the purpose of worship and honor. In other words, the apostle John was in the presence of God. He worshipped God when the Holy Spirit supernaturally brought him to holy ground, to see and hear from the glorified Christ. Thank God for the Holy Spirit because he always sets the stage for worship!

Listen, friends: worship sets the stage for you to hear something from God. John said while he was in the Spirit on the Lord's Day that he heard a "voice." Worship prepares the believers spiritual inner ear, to hear the spiritual voice of God. This voice was so captivating, so intriguing, that it influenced John to turn around to see what was going on; the voice was so powerful that John had to turn around and see where it was coming from.

I have two things that I would like to say on this; first, every sincere believer that spends quality time with Christ knows the voice of Christ. Jesus said, "My sheep, hear my voice" (John 10:27). Second, the voice of Christ will make you or influence you to turn to him and away from sin. The prophet Isaiah said, "Turn to me and be saved, all the ends of the earth! For I am God and there is no other" (Isa. 45:22, ESV).

When John heard the voice of Christ, it was loud as a trumpet. He then noticed seven golden lampstands, and in the middle of the lampstands stood one like the Son of Man—Jesus. The lampstands represent Christ and the Church as lights to the world (Matt. 5:16, John 8:12).

This man had on a long, flowing robe that reached down to his feet, and around his chest was a golden girdle; the girdle represents Christ as being righteous and true. His dress represents him as the great high priest (Exod. 28:2–4). John heard Christ say that he was the alpha and omega, the first and the last, and then instructed him to write what he sees in a book and then send it to the seven Churches, which are in Asia. These Churches would include Ephesus, Smyrna, Pergamos, Thyatira, Sardis, Philadelphia, and Laodicea.

As John, the beloved disciple, looked at him who was like that of the Son of Man, he described his head and hair. He said that it was white like wool and white as snow. The description that John saw is in reference of Christ being around a long time, even before time, as we know it existed. It speaks of Christ's eternity. Daniel 7:9 states, "I beheld till the thrones were cast down, and the Ancient of days did sit, whose garment was white as snow, and the hair of his head like the pure wool: his throne was like the fiery flame, and his wheels as burning fire."

Again, I say, Christ is eternal. He is alpha and omega, the beginning and the end. Before there was a *when* or *where*, before there was a heaven or an earth, there was God! I would also add that since Christ is the Ancient of days that he is a God full of understanding and wisdom. He is omniscient; he is all knowing.

This gives me great joy and comfort because I serve a God that knows all things. John then describes the eyes of the one he saw; he says that his eyes were as flames of fire. This is to say that Christ has the ability to see behind man's deeds and motives, that his eyes are so penetrating that there is nothing that Christ can't see. Solomon said, "The eyes of the Lord are in every place, beholding the evil and the good" (Prov 15:3). He sees what's going on in his Churches, and he sees what's going on in the lives of his individual followers. When I was in elementary school, I would sometimes walk the train tracks that was located in front of the school. One day, as I began to walk by them to go home, my friend and I noticed that there was a nonmoving train with an empty caboose. When we noticed that no one was around, we decided to go into the caboose to explore. To our surprise we noticed that there were flares in a certain area, and it was as if the flares were calling our name for us to pick them up, so they could go home with us. We both gave in to the temptation and were more than willing to ablige their call. We took the flares and headed home. When I arrived at my home, an uneasy feeling of conviction came upon me. I thought that even though no one saw us take the flares, that it was all right, but God saw us and he was not pleased with what I had done. I immediately ran back to the caboose and returned the flares. That was a perfect example of Proverbs 15:3. God's eyes are in every place, and He sees the good and the bad deeds of mankind. When one has a relationship with Christ and errs into sin, God witnesses this wrongdoing and convicts the person with the Holy Spirit, so that the person can repent from wrongdoing and can right the wrong. The writer of the book of Hebrews said, "For whom the Lord loveth he chasteneth every son whom he receiveth" (Heb 12:6).

John then said that the one who looks like the Son of Man has feet like unto fine brass. The description of fine brass or polished brass is symbolic of Christ's divine judgment. When Christ died on the cross, the judgment of our sins was placed upon him. He was a judge for our sins. He paid the debt by the shedding of his blood on Calvary's cross (Heb 9:22).

The prophet Isaiah said, "But he was wounded for our transgressions, he was bruised for our iniquities: the chastisement of our peace was upon him; and with his stripes we are healed. All we like sheep have gone astray, we have turned everyone to his own way; and the Lord hath laid on him the iniquity of us all" (Isa. 53:5–6).

When John writes of Christ's voice as the sound of many waters, he was speaking about the authority that Christ has and that was given to him by his Father. It is with great authority that when he speaks things happen, and people will know that it is out of the ordinary. Matter of fact, when Jesus spoke to the boisterous winds to calm down the Sea of Galilee, his disciples said, "What manner of man is this, that even the winds and the sea obey him?" (Matt. 8:27).

In the book of Genesis, we read how the authoritative voice of God was spoken, and the result of it was the creation of heaven and earth. Friends, I will have you to know that the authoritative voice of Christ can penetrate the boundaries of death and bring forth life. Jesus called Lazarus from a prison of death by the anointed authority of his voice, and he came back alive! (John 11:43–44). Yes, friends, things happen when the authoritative voice of Christ speaks!

As we approach verse 16, John says that Christ held seven stars in his right hand, and from his mouth went a two-edged sword. The seven stars represent the seven angels or messengers to each of the seven Churches. This would be the pastors of the Churches, since they are the earthly shepherds that are responsible for the shepherding and for preaching of the gospel message to the church.

The two-edged sword is the Word of God that penetrates the very heart of man. The Word of God is so sharp, that as it is preached, it cuts with conviction, magnifying the areas of life that need to be changed and corrected. The apostle Paul said, "All scripture is given by the inspiration of God, and is profitable for doctrine, for reproof, for correction, for instruction in righteousness" (2 Tim 3:16).

The writer of the book of Hebrews said, "For the Word of God is quick, and powerful, and sharper than any two-edged sword, piercing even to the dividing asunder of soul and spirit, and of the joints and marrow, and is a discerner of the thoughts and intents of the heart" (Heb 4:12). John also speaks of his appearance. He said, "his countenance was as the sun shineth in his strength" (Rev. 1:16).

This speaks of Christ's splendor, his radiant glory. Christ's brilliance is so bright that it is compared to the sun in the sky. As you know, the sun is so powerfully bright that no man can gaze upon it for a long length of time. However, it gives light, warmth, and life to all on earth. So it is, and more with the radiant glory of Christ, for truly it gives life, hope, and light to all who are under the umbrella of his love. John said, "In him was life; and the life was the light of men" (John 1:4). David said, "For with thee is the fountain of life: in thy light, shall we see light" (Psalm 36:9). Jesus said, "I am the light of the world: he that followeth me shall not walk in darkness" (John 8:12).

The light that John saw upon Christ was so powerful that it causes him to fall down like he was dead. Listen, friends, no one can remain standing after experiencing the anointed presence of Christ in his full glory. When the Glory of the Lord was shining over the tabernacle in the wilderness, Moses was not allowed to go into a tent because the glory of the Lord filled the tent. It wasn't until the cloud lifted that Moses was permitted to go into the tabernacle (Ex 40:34–36).

Yes, friends, the anointed glory of the Lord is powerful! When John fell uncontrollably to the ground, Christ laid his right hand upon him and said, "Fear not: I am the first and the last" (Rev.17). What does this mean? Let's see if we can find some understanding of this verse. First of all, when Christ laid his hand upon John, it is to show endearment and comfort.

Remember, the awesome presence of Christ was so terrifyingly strong and powerful that it paralyzed John to the point that he fainted. John's finite mind was not able to comprehend or make sense out of what was happening to him, so just like a computer or power grid that gets overloaded, he just shut down. However, with care and comfort, Jesus laid his hand upon John and rebooted him back for service.

Second, Jesus tells him to fear not because he is the "first and the last." This is to say that Christ was comforting him through the longevity of his proven power. John had no need to worry or fear because he was with Christ, and he was going to be with him always, even until the end of time. The Psalmist says, "Before the mountains were brought forth, or ever thou hadst formed the earth and the world, even from everlasting to everlasting, thou art God" (Ps. 90:2). The word *everlasting* in Hebrew is, עוֹלָם/ *'olam*, and it translates as *always, evermore, perpetual*, and "to be in continuous existence." This is good to know because God is a God that will always be in existence. He does not fade away like fashion, like outdated clothes, or like furniture. He will always be there for us, even until the end of the world (Matt. 28:20b).

Continuing on to verse 18, Christ introduces himself to John and clears up any doubt of his living existence. He says, "I am he that liveth, and was dead; and, behold, I am alive for evermore, Amen." This statement speaks of Christ as the ultimate atonement of sin. It reminds us of his redemptive work of salvation; it reminds us of the cross and how his shedded blood validates our justification in him. Yes, our salvation was signed, sealed, and delivered when he rose from the dead. Yes, beloved, we have been declared righteous by the resurrection of Jesus Christ. By writing to show the spiritual value as well as its significance on how believers are justified through Christ, let's define the word justified in the Greek. It is the word δικαιόω / dikaioō, meaning to render free or innocent or to be declared righteous. Notice what the Apostle Paul said when he spoke of Christ's resurrection and how it sealed our righteous standing in him. He said, "Who was delivered for our offences, and was raised again for our jurisdiction" (Romans 4:25). He also said, "Therefore being justified by faith, we have peace with God through our Lord Jesus Christ" (Romans 5:1). On a personal note, I get so excited when I think about how Christ atoned for our sins. It's a volcanic joy that erupts continuously in my soul. Yes! When I think about how I was set free, how I was acquitted of my sins and declared righteous in him, tears of joy flow down like lava with a burning desire to serve him with love and gratitude. He died for me. He took my black sins and turned them white as snow. He lives and was resurrected by God the Father for you and me.

This is an important truth because this statement clears up any doubt about Christ still being dead. It's an important truth because it separates Christ from any other gods that they say exist. Christ is the only God that rose from the grave and still lives, and he will remain alive forevermore. It's an important truth because if Christ was not raised from the dead, then our preaching would be in vain, and we as believers would still be in sin.

Notice the truthful statements of Paul, when he said, "And if Christ be not risen, then is our preaching vain, and your faith is also vain. Yea and we are found false witnesses of God; because we have testified that he raised up Christ: whom he raised not up, if so be that the dead rise not. For if the dead rise not, then is not Christ raised: And if Christ be not raised, your faith is vain; ye are yet in your sins. Then they also which are fallen asleep in Christ are perished" (1 Cor 15:14–18).

Christ then tells John that he has the keys of hell and of death. This statement let us know that Christ has power and authority over death and hell.

When Christ raised Lazarus from the dead, it showed that he was the resurrection and the life, that he has power over death. When God the Father raised Christ from the dead, it showed that he has power and authority over the grave and death. He will also be the one who will determine who will spend eternity in hell. John said, "And whosoever was not found written in the book of life was cast into the lake of fire" (Rev. 20:15).

It's a blessing to know that hell is the one place that believers don't have to worry about going. You may ask why. It is because with that same authority is given eternal life to all who accept him as Lord and Savior. The apostle Paul said, "The wages of sin is death, but the gift of God is eternal life" (Rom 6:23).

Christ instructed John to write down the things that he had seen, the things that are, and the things that shall be hereafter. First, what significant things did John see? He saw the risen and glorified Christ. He is alpha and the omega, the beginning and the end. He is the first and the last.

John was to write down what he had seen within the vision of what he saw. The things that are, are the things that were going on in the seven Churches of Asia. Let us also note that the things that were going on in those Churches are some of the practices that are going on in our twenty-first century's Church. Remember, it was Christ who walked in the middle of the seven golden candlesticks, and he noticed the practices that were going on. Who can escape from the all-seeing eyes of Christ?

Now the things that shall be hereafter are the things that will take place after the Rapture of the Church, the tribulation period, the marriage of the Lamb, the millennium, and the prophetic eternal state with God—to name just a few of the apocalyptical events.

John, in his dialogue with Christ, closes this 1st chapter out by the explanations of the seven stars and the seven golden candlesticks. Again, like I explained before, the seven stars are symbolic of the seven angels or the seven pastors of the Churches, whereas the seven golden candlesticks are symbolic of the seven Churches.

Let me also add that even though seven Churches are mentioned in the text, it also represents all of the body of Christ, which is the universal Church. Simply because there were things that were practiced within those Churches that were against God's will, and there were also things that were pleasing in his sight. Either way, the things were to be written down so that the body of Christ can either correct or find encouragement to continue to work the works of him that has sent us; for when night, cometh, no man can work (John 9:4).

2:1–7

As we begin chapter 2, the beloved disciple addressed the angel (pastor) of the Church of Ephesus. He reminds them that it is Christ who holds all pastors or spiritual messengers in his hands. This is good to know for the Church because Satan is really after the pastors. He tries to attack them in all areas of their life, trying to hinder them from being effective leaders of the Church.

How many times have we heard or read about certain pastors within our local community who have been caught up in some type of sinful scandal? If it's not adultery, it's theft; if it's not theft, it's sexual molestation—to name just a few. Satan's main objective is to dethrone God's leaders so that the sheep will scatter.

When this happens, it brings shame upon the Church, and then the Church loses its effectiveness. However, these types of satanic attacks can be resisted if only pastors remind themselves of who is able to keep them from falling. Christ is able to hold all Christians by the strength of his mighty hand. However, Pastors, as well as lay Christians, must be willing to be kept by Christ during their times of temptations and weakness.

John then reminds the Pastors of the Church of Ephesus that Christ knows what is going on in all of his Churches. He says that Christ walks in the midst of the seven golden candlesticks. Again, the seven golden candlesticks are the seven Churches of Asia Minor (Turkey), which is symbolic of all Churches that represent and live a lifestyle holy unto him.

Pastors must watch carefully the religious practices that go on within the body of the Church, simply because not all practices glorify Christ. All works and religious practices must bring honor and glory to God. If this does not happen, then those who do such practices seek to bring attention to themselves, which is self-idolatry.

Christ starts out by commending the Church of Ephesus by saying, "I know thy works, and thy labour and thy patience."

It should be the believers lifestyle and commitment to work righteous works before Christ. The Church of Ephesus performed righteous works unto Christ in the beginning, but then as time went on, they were losing the fire of putting Christ first. They were commended by Christ for their labor. The word for *labor* in Greek is the word κοπος/*kopos*, meaning to beat the breast with grief or sorrow, trouble, labor, toil, and weariness.

The Church of Ephesus suffered for the work of Christ; they felt weariness as they toiled for Christ. They felt grief and sorrow as they labored in Christ's name. Through all of this, Christ noticed their patience. The Greek word for *patience* is the word υπομονη/*hupo-*

mone, meaning "to persevere," *endurance*, or *steadfastness*. Christ saw how they were persevering as they labored to build up the Kingdom of God. Christ commended them for not putting up with those who were evil—they would not continue with them; they would not endure or agree with them.

The believers of Ephesus tested the so-called apostles. They asked them if they had seen Christ, and if their answer was no, they would not even listen to what they had to say; they would even ask them to leave town. Even though the Church of Ephesus suffered while they worked for Christ, they did not faint in the work of Christ. They kept on persevering in Christ's work.

Listen, friends. Because of the opposition, you may get weary and weak at times when you work for Jesus, but the opposition should never quench the love that you have for the work. After Christ commended the Church of Ephesus for the works of faith that he saw in them, he then rebuked them for leaving their first love. Well, you may ask, how can a Church who just received good spiritual commendations for Christ leave their first love, which is Christ and the work of the ministry?

To explain this, let us seek the Greek meaning of the word *left*. It is the word *αφιημι/aphiemi*, meaning to go away leaving, or to bid going away of a husband divorcing his wife. The Church of Ephesus had not as of yet completely left Christ; they were, however, on their way. They had become distracted with the things they were going on in the city of Ephesus.

In other words, the intimate and close relationship that they had once had was now being over shadowed by the beauty and wealth of the city. Their intense enthusiasm for the work of Christ was fading like the sun that hides itself beyond the horizon. Beloved, it is your responsibility to keep the fire of loving Christ hot around the center of your heart. If you don't, you will find your love for Christ replaced by things of vanity.

Don't get so caught up in the religion of having Church that you forget that Jesus is the reason for the service. Don't get so caught up with the beauty of the world that you forget and become sidetracked of knowing that God was the one who created the world. Despite

Ephesus falling away, Jesus reached out to them and invited them to repent of their sin. Christ asked the Church of Ephesus, "Remember therefore from whence thou art fallen and repent."

Christ tells the Church to remember how their love was in the beginning when the coals of evangelism were hot and their love for him was paramount. He tells them to repent and turn away from those things that distracted them and come back to him like they were when they first heard and accepted the message of the gospel. Christ then tells the Church of Ephesus that if they didn't repent, that he was going to remove their candlestick from its place.

Christ uses the word *repent* again to show the importance and urgency of the matter. By Christ saying that he would remove their candlestick is to be taken that the Church of Ephesus would lose its effectiveness in winning souls to Christ. Remember that the saints and the Church are the lights of the world; it's our responsibility to shine for Christ so that the unsaved may come into the saving knowledge of Christ and give him glory.

After Christ rebukes the Church of Ephesus because they were in the process of leaving him and his works, he then commends them again for hating the deeds of the Nicolaitans. Who were the Nicolaitans? The Nicolaitans were a so-called Christian sect that taught that in order to learn about sin and immorality, one must experience it. Especially when it came down to fornication and eating foods that they were offering to idols. There religious belief was no more than a cult that tried to influence the church of Ephesus away from their first love, which is Christ.

Christ then invites all believers who have spiritual understanding to hear. Not only must they hear the message, but as they depend on the Holy Spirit for his leading and direction, they should comply with what the message is saying to them as the Church. Christ promises to give to those who overcome an invitation to eat from the tree of life that is located in the midst of the paradise of God.

This is to say that that all born-again believers who live and work for Christ will be in heaven enjoying the fruit of the tree of life. We don't know, however, what type of fruit it will be, or what benefit it would be for us. However, anything that comes from God has to be good, for God made all things good, and if I would speculate, it will be so good to the incorruptible body that it will benefit our worship to God.

2:8-11

Christ then turns his attention from the Church of Ephesus and addressed the Church of Smyrna. Christ has nothing but praise and commendation for the Church of Smyrna. He begins by telling the angel/pastor of the Church that he is the first and the last meaning. That he, Christ, existed before all things. By saying he is the last is to say he is God of eternity. Christ then encouraged them by saying he was dead and is now alive.

This was soothing to the believers' faith because they were being persecuted and even put to death for the sake of Christ. Since there were some who died for the gospel like Christ, they also were to live again, just like Christ. Christ knew their works, their tribulation, and their poverty. The Greek word for *work* is the word εργον/*ergon*, meaning *work, deeds, labor,* or *business*. Christ knew how faithful they were working for him. They were about the business of building up the Kingdom of God. He knew about the tribulation that they were in. The Greek word for *tribulation* is the word θλιψις/*thlipsis* meaning *trouble, anguish, persecution,* and *affliction*. However, the trouble or persecution that they were in was not the Great Tribulation.

They were being persecuted by the Roman Empire. Christ also knew their poverty. The Greek word is πτωχεια/*ptocheia* meaning *poverty, beggary,* and "the condition of one destitute of riches and abundance." In other words, the Church of Smyrna lacked resources. But nevertheless, Christ commended them and told them that they were spiritually rich. Just like Christ who knew the faithful works of the Church of Smyrna, he knew those Jews who said they were Jews but were not on the inside. They worshipped Satan; they were not a part of God's family.

Christ tells them not to fear, and we know by history that this is what strengthens their faith, for many went to their death singing praises unto the Lord; many were put into prison because of their faith in Jesus, but their faith helped them overcome their fears. Last week a city clerk was jailed because she refused to give out marriage applications to same-sex couples. She said to do this was to go against her religious convictions. However, by the prayers of the Church, the woman was set free.

Christ then encouraged them by saying, "Be thou faithful unto death and I will give thee a crown of Life." We don't know what this crown is. However, we do know that it's a reward given by God for a life of faithful service. James said, "Blessed is the man that endureth temptation, for when he is tried, he shall receive the crown of life, which the Lord hath promised to them that love him" (James 1:12).

Again, Christ says that if you hear and understand the message that the Spirit is conveying to his Church and do them, they will not have to worry about being punished in hell, which is the second death.

2:12-17

As we continue with the Church of Pergamos the letter, as always, is addressed to the angel/pastor of the Church. The source of this letter comes from him who has the sharp sword with two edges.

The sword with two edges is the Word of God (Heb 4:12), and it cuts and exposes all unrighteousness. The Church of Pergamos was a worldly church, a Church of false religion, and Christ has a word of warning for them. But first of all, he commends the Church for being located where they are. It's not easy doing ministry in an area where Satan rules. Remember, the city of Pergamos was a city of false religion. Matter of fact, they even had a temple of Caesar Augustus, which some worshipped. They had an altar for the Greek God Zeus, as well as the temple of Dionysius, which is the same as Bacchus, the god of wine and alcohol.

But nevertheless, the Church of Pergamos held on to their faith and would not deny the name of Jesus. Matter of fact, there was a man named Antipas who died for his convictions in Christ. It is said that Antipas was the first Christian martyr of the Church of

Pergamos. After Christ commands them, he then tells them that he has a few things that he has against them.

First, he was against them because there were those among them who held to the doctrine of Balaam. It was a teaching that said it was okay to marry into the Moabite nation, a doctrine that was against the will of God. This teaching introduced them into the sin of idolatry and fornication. They were also those who held on to the doctrine of the Nicolaitans, which says it's okay to indulge in certain sins and experience them. Christ tells them to repent, or he will come unto them quickly and will fight against them with the sword of his mouth.

In other words, the only remedy for their wickedness is to repent before God and confess their sins. The Greek word for *repent* is the word, *μετανοεω/metanoeo*, meaning "a change of mind" or to "change one's mind for the better." The Word of God says this about confessing sin. It says, "If we confess our sins, he is faithful and just to forgive us our sins, and to cleanse us from all unrighteousness" (1 John 1:9).

If the Church of Pergamos did not repent, then Christ would come unto them quickly and fight against them with the sword of his mouth. This is to be interpreted as the wrath of God or being at war with his word. It's not a good idea to be at war with God's Word. It was God's Word that was spoken to create the world; it was God's Word that was spoken to bring about healing to the centurion soldier. Think how bad it would be if God speaks his authoritative and powerful word against those who do not repent from their sins.

Christ then tells the Church of Pergamos that if they would hear what the spirit is saying to the Churches and overcome the temptations of the world, that Christ will give them the hidden manna. Well, this is to say that when believers allow the Holy Spirit to lead them in every facet of their lives, especially when it comes to not yielding to sin, that Christ will be with them to give them bread that feeds the soul—which is imperative for spiritual growth.

Notice what John, the beloved disciple, says of Christ: "Then Jesus said unto them, Verily, verily, I say unto you, Moses gave you not that bread from heaven; but my Father giveth you the true bread from heaven. For the bread of God is he which cometh down from heaven, and giveth life unto the world. Then said they unto him, Lord, evermore give us this bread. And Jesus said unto them, I am the bread of life: he that cometh to me shall never hunger; and he that beliveth on me shall never thirst" (John 6:32–35). Peter said, "But grow in grace, and in the knowledge of our Lord and Savior Jesus Christ. To him be glory both now and forever. Amen" (2 Peter 3:18).

Christ is the "hidden manna." The world (unbelievers) do not know him. Sin and unbelief have hidden the unbeliever from the true deity of Christ; their sins have hid Christ's face from them (Isa. 59:1–2). Satan has blinded their eyes from accepting him as the "way and the truth" (John 14:6). Paul said, "In whom the god of this world hath blinded the minds of them which believe not, lest the light of the glorious gospel of Christ, who is the image of God, should shine unto them" (2 Cor 4:4). As believers of Christ, we must feed daily upon Jesus. He is the true manna; He is the true wonder bread that does wonders for our life and soul.

Christ then tells the angel of the Church of Pergamos that he will give them a white stone, and written on the stone will be a new name. This will be a name that is between Christ and the believer. As to the white stone, stones were given to intimate friends with names engraved upon them to show their close and private relationship.

2:18–29

We now come to the Church of Thyatira and the message that Christ has for them.

The city of Thyatira was another city that was well built and fortified, but instead of it being built on mountains, it was built in a valley on the top of a raised hill. What made the city strong against attacks were Roman soldiers that were stationed there.

The city was also called the headquarters for many ancient businesses, such as pottery business, tanner business, weaver business, and the business of making of robes as well as the business of dyeing. Matter of fact, Lydia, the businesswoman who sold purple material in Philippi, was from there. Lydia was also Paul's first person that he saved by sharing the gospel of Jesus Christ.

As Christ tells John to write to the Church of Thyatira, he clears up any and all questions, if there are any, about the person behind these fourth coming instructions. It is of course Jesus, who introduces himself as "the Son of God," a title of Christ that is only mentioned once in this book. As John writes, he tells the Church of Thyatira that Jesus's eyes are like unto a flame of fire, and that his feet are like unto fine brass. This of course is a repeat of words that are found in Revelation 1:14–15.

It is good to note that when phrases of scripture are repetitive that it is to show the significance of the content that is being said. Here the symbolism of the content matter is to show without doubt that Christ is not only the Savior, but that he is also an all-knowing and all-seeing judge. In other words, Christ is judging the Church of Thyatira.

It is with the flames of his penetrating eyes that he notices and inspects every work that is against the true nature of his will. With these penetrating and flaming eyes, Christ can see all the hidden and dark places in which this Church exhibited. His feet, which were likened unto fine brass, are symbolic of the coming judgment of what he saw.

This should remind and warn all believers of Christ, who make up the Church, that Christ takes note and will judge all works that is done unto him by Christians. Paul says this of God, "Who will render to every man according to his deeds" (Rom 2:6). Paul also said, "For we must all appear before the judgment seat of Christ; that every one may receive the things done in his body, according to that he hath done, whether it be good or bad" (2 Cor 5:10). Solomon said, "I said in mine heart, God shall judge the righteous and the wicked: for there is a time there for every purpose and for every work" (Eccl 3:17).

I tell you, believers, scriptures such as these should make every Christian strive to walk the narrow road of righteousness and holiness. Now, getting back to the Church of Thyatira, John writes to tell them that Christ says that he knows their works, their charity, their service, their faith, and their patience, and again he says their works. He also says to them that their last works are more important than the first. Notice that Christ commanded the Church of Thyatira six times to draw attention to their intimate relationship that they had with Christ.

Listen, believers, if you love Christ you will serve him; you will work to build up his kingdom, but if you don't love him with your whole heart, you will rebel against him and you will never work for him. Jesus said, "Why call ye me Lord, Lord and do not the things which I say?" (Luke 6:46). James said, "Yea, a man may say, thou hast faith, and I have works: shew me thy faith without thy works, and I will shew thee my faith by my works" (Jas 2:18).

Even though Christ commends Thyatira for having works of virtue, he rebukes them for tolerating Jezebel for teaching that the sin of fornication was all right for believers to do. This Jezebel that he speaks about was no other than a self-proclaimed prophetess that was teaching false doctrine within their Church. If you could remember, Jezebel implemented pagan practices into the kingdom of Israel. She was wicked and immoral.

They were also rebuked for eating food that was sacrificed to idols. Therefore, Christ tells the Church of Thyatira that this false prophetess has the spirit of a woman who led the Northern Kingdom into sin. Listen, believers, in order for the Church to shine and grow for Christ, it must lay aside every sin and weight that cause believers to fall from the grace of God. Matter of fact, the Bible teaches us to come out from among them and mark them who are against the will of God. Paul said, "Wherefore come out from among them, and be ye separate, saith the Lord, and touch not the unclean thing; and I will receive you" (2 Cor 6:17).

Paul also said, "Now I beseech you brethren, mark them which cause division and offences contrary to the doctrine which ye have learned; and avoid them" (Rom 16:17). Christ tells the Church of Thyatira that he gave this false teacher, as well as this false system of religious doctrine plenty of time to repent, but because of a rebellious heart, she (heretics and their teachings) refused the true doctrine of the gospel, and furthermore they are still in their sins. But nevertheless, Christ tells those who believe to hold on their faith until he receives them unto himself.

Christ tells them that if they hold out until he comes and overcomes the seducing teachings of this false teacher, that he will give them power over the nations. By this he meant that a time was coming for all believers who endure to the end of time that they would be in the Rapture and then rule in his millennial kingdom in a position of authority with him for a thousand years. Christ says that he would give them that morning star. Who is this star? It's Jesus the Christ. Those believers who endure until the end would be in the divine presence of Christ forevermore. Matter of fact, friends, we should look forward to that blessed and wonderful day. Titus said, "Looking for that blessed hope, and the glorious appearing of the great God and our Savior Jesus Christ" (Titus 2:13).

Those believers who make it their business to hear the voice of the Holy Spirit and apply what he is saying to the Churches will be blessed.

3:1-6

John the Revelator now writes and informs us of the Church of Sardis. However, before we address the spiritual condition of the Church, let us look at the history of the city. The city itself was one of the oldest cities in Asia Minor (Western Turkey), and it was the capital, Lydia. It was a rich and prosperous city that was well-known for manufacturing wool, jewelry, coins, and carpets. As a matter of fact, it was known as the carpet city of the world. The city was becoming so prosperous because of its trade that their population grew in number as well as their various businesses. It became so prosperous because of its trade that a second city had to be built to sustain the increase of their population. The original city, which was located on an elevated plateau of the Hermus valley, was no longer suited to sustain their growth. As far as their worshipped practices, the people of the city worship the Greek gods Apollo and Cybele (Diana), and according to Greek mythology, they were brother and sister. Apollo was the god of the sun, and Diana was the goddess of nature, but in

Ephesus, she was known as the goddess of fertility. As time passed, the city was destroyed by an earthquake. However, the temple ruins of Apollo and Cybele can still be seen to this day. Let us move forward now and discuss the Church of Sardis. Again, the addressee of the letter was to the angel (pastor or messenger) of the Church of Sardis. John says that the one who is speaking to the pastor of the Church of Sardis is the one who hath the seven spirits of God.

This phrase is to be interpreted as Christ sending out the Holy Spirit into the world in its fullness. Again, the seven stars are the seven pastors of the Churches of Asia. Sardis as you know is included in this number and therefore it is to be taken that Christ is giving the message to the pastor of the Church of Sardis. Christ commends them for their works of the Christian faith; however, He condemns them because their works had no life within it. They were just going about the motions and practices of faith, but they had no inward connection with Christ.

In other words, they appeared to be lively and zealous in doing Christian service, but on the inside, they were dead. Jesus once told the scribes and Pharisees the same things about their religious works. He said, "Woe unto you, scribes and Pharisees, hypocrites! For ye are like unto white sepulchers, which indeed appear beautiful outward, but are within full of dead men's bones, and all uncleanness Even so ye also outwardly appear righteous unto men, but within ye are full of hypocrisy and iniquity" (Matt. 23:27–28).

John writes that Christ said to them to wake up and strengthen the things that remain, because that little faith that they have is about to die. Christ tells them to wake up because it was two times in their history when they were defeated because of them not being able to stay awake and alert to watch the gate of the city from attack. One instance was in 529 BC, when the guards were asleep at their post, and this allowed Cyrus guards to come in and defeat them. And the second instance was in 218 BC, when Antiochus the Great captured the city because of carelessness. It is very important for the twenty-first-century Church to stay awake and focus as well. The apostle Paul said, "Awake to righteous, and sin not, for some have not the knowledge of God: I speak this to your shame" (1 Cor. 15: 34).

Christ then told the Church of Sardis to remember what they heard in the beginning when they first received the gospel and held on to it dearly because if they didn't, they were about to die spiritually. My Christian friends, we must be very careful not to allow our adversary, the devil, to sidetrack us from the teachings of Christ.

The same gospel that we heard and believed when we first receive salvation is the same gospel that will keep us focused on serving Christ. We must meditate day and night so that the spiritual roots of our foundation will never be moved from the doctrine of Christ. The apostle Paul said it best when he said, "Therefore, my beloved brethren, be ye steadfast, unmovable, always abounding in the work of the Lord, forasmuch as ye know that your labour is not in vain in the Lord" (1 Cor 15:58).

After Christ condemns the Church of Sardis for their dead works, he mentioned that there were some believers of that Church who didn't allow their walk of faith to be defiled. Matter of fact, those who have kept the faith will walk with Christ dressed in white to show the genuine purity of their faith and works in Christ. To go along with that, Christ promised never to blot out their name from the book of life.

This does not mean that Christ can and will take someone out of the book of life after their names have been written in; it is to be interpreted as one who genuinely accepts Christ as Lord. The believing person would never have to worry about their name being removed from the book of life. Jesus said, "And I give unto them eternal life; and they shall never perish, neither shall any man pluck them out of my hand" (John 10:28).

John closes out the message of Christ by saying to the Church of Sardis, "He that hath an ear let him hear what the Spirit saith unto the Churches." It is important for all believers to hear and understand the message of Christ. It is also imperative for them to listen to the Holy Spirit attentively, for in him is the insightful treasures of God that enable believers to grow spiritually strong in their faith. Christ promises to all the faithful who confess him to be Lord, that he will confess them to his Father in heaven. Beloved, what a day of rejoicing that will be for us as the people of God. This day will trump all days of accolades and achievements. It will surpass all ceremonial days of joy, when names of the righteous are called in public to receive the crown of life to commemorate a life of service to God on earth. I mean, can you imagine Christ confessing your name before God the Father in the midst of his glorified angels?

I remember when I received my undergraduate degree, as well as my graduate degree. When the president of the college and seminary called my name to receive my degrees in the midst of hundreds of people, my heart leaped with joys of excitement. I was so overwhelmed with elation that I almost teared up with joy. You may ask why. Because I thought about all the long nights of study that I had to do to get this diploma. I thought about all the papers that I had to write to get to this point. The joy and excitement that I received when I walked across that stage after I heard my name called cannot take the place when Christ confessed me before our Father God in heaven. Hallelujah! What a day of rejoicing that would be.

3:7-13

John, the beloved disciple, now turns his attention to the Church of Philadelphia. Christ, through John, tells this Church about his divine character. He tells them that he is holy. The Greek word for holy is άγιος/*hagios,* meaning *saint, holy one,* or "to be different." The Greek word for *true* is the word αληθινος/*alethinos,* meaning *genuine, real,* or "the opposite of what is fictitious, counterfeit, imaginary, simulated, or pretended." John, the beloved disciple, then says of Christ that he has the key of David and that Christ has the authority to open and close doors.

When that happens, no one can reopen them, and no one can close them. In my opinion, Christ having all this authority over his Churches is to say that he has the authority to shut down ministries and Churches that are not seeking or doing his divine will. Also, this statement is to interpreted as Christ as being the divine ruler of the universe as well as the King of Kings, who will reign over the house of Jacob during his millennium kingdom (Isaiah 22:22, Luke 1:32–33).

The city of Philadelphia, meaning brotherly love, was named after Attalus Philadelphus II. It was he who founded the city. Philadelphus was also the king of Pergamos. It was a name given to the city because Philadelphus was shown love and loyalty by his brother Eumenes. Philadelphia was located twenty-five miles south of Sardis, and its modern name is Allah Sher (city of God).

The Church of Philadelphia, like the Church of Sardis, received not one rebuke from the Lord Christ. Why? You may ask. Because the Church of Philadelphia was a Church that believed in the Word of God. This Church was also set in a city full of paganism. But they still hung on to the deep convictions of God's Word, which motivated them to cling to God's Word.

My Christian friends, what a difference our cities would be if only they stood loyal to the Word of God. What a better world this would be if only the Word of God became first and foremost in the lives of the people. Solomon said, righteousness exalts a nation, but sin is a reproach to any people (Prov. 14:34).

Christ commends the Church of Philadelphia for their seven acts of genuine service. (1) He commends them for their works. The Church of Philadelphia was a Church that lived what they preached. They were a Church that remains faithful to their religious conviction.

They were a Church that allowed God's Word to show up in their conversation and lifestyle. Jesus said, "Let your light so shine before men that they may see your good works and glorify the Father which is in heaven" (Matt. 5:16). The apostle Paul encourages all churches by saying, "For we are his workmanship, created in Christ Jesus unto good works, which God hath before ordained that we should walk in them" (Ephesians 2:10).

Listen, faithful and true witnesses of God, true followers of Christ not only hear God's Words, but they also do God's Words as well. James said, "Wherefore lay apart all filthiness and superfluity of naughtiness, and receive with meekness the engrafted word, which is able to save your souls. But be ye doers of the word, and not hearers only, deceiving your own selves. But if any be a hearer of the word, and not a doer, he is like unto a man beholding his natural face in a glass: For he that beholdeth himself, and goeth his way, and straightway forgetteth what manner of man he was. But whoso looketh in the perfect law of liberty, and continueth therein, he being not a forgetful hearer, but a doer of the word, this man shall be blessed in his deeds" (Jas 1:21–25).

(2) An open door. These words can mean an open door of ministry, an open door of opportunity, or an open door to his knowledge. Or because of their obedience to His word, it could mean an open door of blessing. The Psalmist said, "No good thing will he withhold from them that walk uprightly" (Psalm 84:11b). Solomon said, "But the upright shall have good things in possession" (Proverbs 28:10c).

(3) For thou hast a little strength. The Church of Philadelphia was commended on the little strength that they had. Listen, it's a blessing to be of great faith and of great strength. However, it's also a blessing to utilize the little faith that one has in the service of the Lord. Even in their weakness, the Church of Philadelphia hung true to God's Word. Jesus said, "For verily I say unto you, if ye have faith as a grain of mustard seed, ye shall say unto this mountain, remove hence to yonder place; and it shall remove; and nothing shall be impossible unto you" (Matt. 17:20).

(4) "And hast kept my word." Again, the Church of Philadelphia lived and applied God's Word to their life. They were true laborers for the Lord Jesus Christ. I can imagine that they not only kept God's Words during good times, but when opposition was against them as well. Paul said, "Therefore, my beloved brethren, be ye steadfast, unmovable, always abounding in the work of the Lord, forasmuch as ye know that your labour is not in vain in the Lord" (1 Cor 15:58).

(5) "And hast not denied my name." What a great testimony! The Church of Philadelphia was a Church that was not ashamed of the gospel of Jesus Christ. They professed and proclaimed that Jesus is Lord. As I look at our world and its many religious belief systems. Every non-Christian is professing that their god is true, their god is the one that is real, and their religion is the right one that brings about satisfaction and completeness to the soul. But nevertheless, Jesus said, "I am the way, the truth, and the life, no man cometh unto the Father, but by me" (John 14:6).

Yes, friends, Christ is looking for a Church that is not ashamed to lift him up in the midst of wickedness and idolatry. Paul said, "I am not ashamed of the gospel of Christ: it is the power of unto salvation to everyone that believeth; to the Jew first, and also to the Greek" (Rom 1:16).

(6) Behold, I will make them to come and worship before thy feet, and to know that I have loved thee." This is to say that the enemies of the Church of Philadelphia, as well as all those who were coming in opposition against this Church, will know that God's love is upon this Church. David said, "When the wicked, even mine enemies and my foes came upon me to eat up my flesh, they stumbled and fell" (Psalm 27:2). David also said, "Thou prepareth a table before me in the presence of mine enemies: thou anointed my head with oil, my cup runneth over" (Psalm 23:5).

(7) "Because thou hast kept the word of my patience." This is to be interpreted as the Church who waits for Christ return to earth patiently. Christ then promises that this Church, as well as all Churches, will be saved from the period of the seven-year tribulation period.

This is what he meant by saying, "I also will keep thee from the hour of temptation, which shall come upon all the world, to try them that dwell upon the earth." It's good to know friends that the Church will be Raptured up to Christ before the Great Tribulation would begin (1 Thess. 4:13–18).

Christ informs the Church to take note and listen to what he is saying. He tells them that he will come back quickly, meaning that he will come back suddenly at an hour that they know not. Also, if they continue to hold on to their faith and live to please Christ, they will be rewarded the crown of life. Christ tells them that if they hold on that he will make them to be a pillar in the temple of God.

In other words, they will be in eternity with Christ forever. They will also receive the new name of Christ to show that they have a close and intimate relationship. Christ closes his remarks to this Church by saying once again, "He that hath an ear, let him hear what the Spirit saith unto the Church."

3:14–22

We will now discuss the last and final Church of Asia Minor, which is the Church of Laodicea. First of all, the city was built by Antiochus II (261–246 BC). He named the city after his wife, Laodice. The city was forty miles southeast of Philadelphia, and they were famous for the manufacture of wool, which made the city rich. It was also the center of banking operations. The people who lived in that area worshipped Asclepius, the healing god.

Christ then tells John to address this letter to the pastor of the Church, and inform him that the message was coming from the amen, the faithful and true witness. By these words, Christ was saying that he establishes all of God the Father's promises. Matter of fact, he is the last word, the ultimate authority, and from this authority comes the final decision of all things. The apostle Paul said this about Christ's authority: "For all the promises of God in him are yea, and in him Amen unto the glory of God by us" (2 Cor 1:20).

Christ also says that he is the faithful and true witness. This is to say that Christ is a reliable and dependable witness of what he had seen and heard from God the Father. His message is true and that he is the one who reveals the truth about God faithfully. The words "the beginning of the creation of God" means that Christ is the origin or the source of all things that was ever created. John said, "All things were made by him; and without him were not anything made that was made" (John 1:3).

Paul said, "For by him were all things created, that are in heaven, and that are in earth, visible, and invisible, whether they be thrones, or dominions, or principalities, or powers: all things were created by him, and for him" (Col 1:16). As we continue, Christ gives no commendation to this Church because they were a Church lifted up in pride and self-satisfaction. They were a Church that was neither cold nor hot. The words *cold* and *hot* depict their service rendered to God. *Cold* to depict them not working at all and *hot* to depict them having great zeal when it comes to rendering Christian service.

Their Christian service to God was lukewarm. Which was a judgment concerning their spiritual condition. This is to be taken that they were lazy and not really serious about Christian service and that Christ was displeased with their half-heartedness. This ineffective condition sickened Christ to the point that he wanted to vomit. In my opinion, the reference of Christ spitting, or vomiting them out of his mouth, means that the church of Laodiceans would lose the effectiveness and not their salvation.

Listen, faithful followers, the Church of Laodiceans represent all those so-called believers who go through life pretending that they are spiritually mature. They look religious on the outside, but on the inside, they are worldly and carnal. Spiritually dead. The Church of Laodicea was a rich and proud Church, and it was the comfort of their wealth that caused Christ to give them a warning of rejection. Verse 17 tells us that the Church of Laodicea depended and looked toward their wealth for security, as opposed to looking and depending on Christ for their eternal security.

They were so comfortable in their richness that they thought they didn't need anything, but what they needed the most was a genuine relationship with Christ. As a mighty counselor, Christ gives them three spiritual principles to correct their lukewarm and lost state. (1) They were to buy from Christ, gold tried in fire. First of all, the words "buy of him" does not mean that Christ is selling salvation. It is to be interpreted as accepting Christ as Savior by faith, in which Christ will give them divine righteousness in return. John the revelator said, "And the Spirit and the bride say Come. And let him that heareth say, Come. And let him that is athirst come. And whoever will, let him take the water of life freely" (Rev. 22:17).

(2) Christ advised them to do this so they can become spiritually rich having white raiment. White raiment depicts genuine Christian service that is pure and undefiled before God. The Psalmist said, "Lord, who shall abide in thy tabernacle? Who shall dwell in thy holy hill? He that walketh uprightly, and worketh righteousness, and speaketh the truth in his heart. He that backbiteth not with his tongue, nor doeth evil to his neighbor, nor taketh up a reproach against his neighbor" (Ps 15:1–3).

The Church of Laodicea was also to anoint their eyes with eye salve in order for them to see. The people of Laodicea anointed their eyes with the eye salve of Asclepius as they rendered worship to their idol god. Christ tells them to anoint their eyes with eye salve to mean that they should depend on the Holy Spirit to open their spiritual eyes of discernment, so they can see the truth behind their spiritual condition, as well as the Kingdom of God.

Christ reminds them that the reason that he chastens them was because of his love for them. Listen, beloved, God is love. He loves the sinner, but he hates the sin. The blessing of grace is open to all. Peter said, "The Lord is not slack concerning his promise, as some men count slackness, but is long suffering to us-ward, not willing that any should perish, but that all should come to repentance" (2 Pet. 3:9).

Christ advises them to repent and turn to him for salvation. He tells them to listen to him because he is knocking at the door of their heart. He tells them to hear his inviting voice, because it's a voice of salvation that guarantees eternal life. He tells them that if they would overcome an unresponsive heart, a lukewarm heart that he will invite him to sit with him and his Father in heaven.

In other words, believers of Christ will reign with him on his blessed glorious throne. What a joyful time we would have when we as the redeemed will come into the presence of the great high priest, the king of kings, and sit next to him for all eternity! What a fellowship, what a joy divine! Thank you, Jesus. Again, Christ closes out his instruction to the Church of Laodicea by allowing the tireless Spirit of God to invite all who have ears to hear what the Spirit is saying to God's Church.

4:1-11

The apostle John finished the earthly instruction of Christ that was given to the seven Churches of Asia Minor and was called up into heaven by the Holy Spirit to view the throne room of God. I received several invitations in my life that I have been invited to. Invitations such as weddings, birthdays, church functions, family functions, retirement functions, and graduation functions, to name but a few. But nevertheless, none of these social gatherings can trump the invitation to see Jesus.

In chapter 4, John was invited to witness the apocalyptic events that were going to transpire on earth. As John was transported into heaven by the Holy Spirit, he saw a door open. This door is symbolic of God granting access to all believers by way of Jesus Christ. Jesus said, "I am the way, the truth, and the life: no man cometh unto get to the Father, but by me" (John 14:6).

John also heard the sound of a trumpet as if it were talking to him. Many theologians have said that this trumpet symbolizes the call and the Rapture of the Church. The apostle Paul said, "Behold, I shew you a mystery, we shall not all sleep, but we shall all be changed, in a moment, in the twinkling of an eye, at the last trump: for the trumpet, shall sound, and the dead shall be raised incorruptible, and we shall be changed" (1 Cor 15:51–52).

It is my belief that that as John was taking up or transported to heaven that this event is to be taken symbolically to show that the earthly Church has been in Raptured or caught up into heaven. We say this because, unlike the nineteen times that the Church was mentioned in chapter 1 to 3, it wasn't mentioned again until chapter 19:7 where the Church appears as the glorious bride of Christ. Also, John said he heard a voice as a sound of a trumpet stating that he should come up hither (4:1).

This trumpet is symbolic of the trumpet that will blow to announce the Rapture of the Church (1 Thess. 4:13–18). Since the Church has been raptured up and is with Christ in heaven, it sets the apocalyptic stage for the Great Tribulation period, which is a time when God judges the earth for seven years.

The Church will have no part in the tribulation period, but before I explain that in detail, let me go back and explain what John saw as the description of God, what John saw as he viewed God's throne room. John said, "And he that sat was to look upon like jasper and a sardine stone: and there was a rainbow round about the throne, in sight like unto an emerald."

Notice that John did not describe a physical appearance of God the Father. God's brilliance was so glorified that John was not able to describe the figure of His shape. The scripture says, "No man has seen God at any time; the only begotten Son, which is in the bosom of the Father, he hath declared him" (John 1:18, 6:46). What came to John's mind to even come close to a description was that of bright, translucent colors of precious gemstones—jasper and carnelian.

To help us see things vividly like John, the Greek word for *jasper* is the word ιασπις/*iaspis*, meaning precious stones of various colors. The brilliant colors would be purple, blue, green, and even clear as crystals. The Greek word for *sardines* is the word σαρδινος/*sardines*, meaning colors of reddish brown or colors of the flesh. John also said that there was a rainbow around the throne of God that reminded him of the color of emerald green.

Also, there appeared around God's throne twenty-four seats, and sitting in them were twenty-four elders clothed in white, and upon their heads were gold crowns. Emanating from God's throne was thunder, lightning, and voices. There were also seven lamps of fire, which are the seven spirits of God.

What does all of that mean? Well, according to *Wilmington's Bible Handbook*, "Some suggest that the 24 elders, who reappear several times in John's vision, were angelic beings. Others believe they may have been a representative body of OT and NT saints (compare 21:12–14). This latter view is suggested by the fact that the Greek word for their crowns is *stephanos*, used elsewhere in the NT to describe the crowns or rewards of victorious believers (see 1 Cor. 9:25; 1 Pet. 5:4), rather than *diadema*, which describes a crown worn by royalty or, in Revelation, by supernatural beings (see 12:3; 13:1; 19:12)." From the perspective that the twenty-four elders are a symbolic representative of the OT body is this: being that there were so many priests to serve in the temple, they could not fulfill their priestly temple obligation without bumping into one another. Therefore, the priests were divided into twenty-four courses to fulfill the religious obligations of the temple (1 Chron. 24:7–18).

After dividing the priests into twenty-four categories or courses, they were then assigned a head leader of each course. They were also called elders of the priests within that group of priests (1 Chron. 24:5). Therefore, it could go without saying that the twenty-four elders in Revelation 4:4 could be symbolically a representative for the twenty-four priests in OT scripture, or it could represent the twelve patriarchs as well as the twelve apostles.

Some see the "seven spirits of God" (4:5, see 1:4) as seven angels. Others view the phrase as a description of the Holy Spirit in his perfection. Verse 5 tells us that out from the throne of God came lighting, thundering, and voices. When I was a child, I was afraid of the lighting and the thundering. Why? You may ask. Because to me, heavy storms always followed; the louder the thunder, the more severe the storm that followed. Therefore, I feel that the thunder and the lighting in this verse is symbolic of God's oncoming-storms of judgment that will be released upon the earth, during the seven years while the Church will be in heaven with Christ for seven years.

To add along with that statement, the thundering and lighting should be taken symbolically to show the awesome presence of God. The Psalmist said, "The voice of thy thunder was in the heaven: the lightings lightened the world: the earth trembled and shook" (Psalm 77:18). Also, when Israel was waiting to receive the laws of God from Moses while he was on Mount Sinai, they saw lighting, and they heard loud thunder and a voice of a loud trumpet coming from the mountain (Ex 19:16).

John also saw a sea of glass like unto crystal, and in the middle of the throne, as well as around the throne, he saw four beasts with eyes in front as well as behind them. What could be the explanation of the sea of glass that John saw?

As I meditated and pondered over that statement, my mind recalled what the Psalmist said in Psalm 148:4. He said, "Praise him, ye heavens of heavens, and ye waters that be above the heavens." Could the waters that be above the waters be the sea of glass that John was referring to? Did John mean that the waters that were around God's throne so clear and pristine that John references them to glass? Could it be that God's throne set his throne in the midst of heavenly water? Was water the foundation of God's throne? The Psalmist said, "Who layeth the beams of his chambers in water: who maketh the clouds his chariot: who walketh upon the wings of the wind" (Ps 104:3).

If this is the case, the only thing that I can say is wow! And that word doesn't even come close to the awesome, supernatural power of God! Or could it mean that the foundation on which God's throne was set was so clear, so pure, and so vast, that it spread out like a sea, which has no end? The four beasts that are mentioned are four living creatures that are very focused and alert as to what was going on.

They resembled the seraphim and the cherubim of Ezekiel's vision, as well as the prophet Isaiah (Ezek. 1:5–10, 10:20; Isa. 6:2–3). As to their symbolic representation, it is my belief that each creature represents one of the four New Testament gospels. The first creature is the lion. Lions as we were told are the king of the jungle. They are fierce, courageous, bold, strong, and powerful. The gospel of Matthew depicts Christ as King. Not only is he King, but he is also the Lord of Lords. Jesus said to the daughter of Zion, "Behold your King is coming to you, Gentle, and mounted on a donkey, even on a colt, the foal of a beast of burden" (Matt. 21:5; Rev. 5:5).

The second living creature that is portrayed is that of an ox, or a cow. An ox is an animal that some farmers would use to plow fields and to carry heavy equipment. They are beasts that are used for the heavy burden of the day. Christ is presented as the suffering servant who carried the burden of sins upon his back.

The third creature, which makes up the four living beasts, is that of a face of a man. The gospel of Luke presents our Lord and Savior as the Son of Man. Jesus said, "The Son of Man is come to seek and to save that which is Lost" (Luke 19:10).

The fourth living beast was compared to a flying eagle." Eagles are symbolic of supremacy and sovereignty. The flying eagle represents Christ's supreme deity. He is sovereign, and there is none like him. He has preeminence. The apostle Paul said in reference to Christ, "Who is the image of the invisible God, the firstborn of every creature. For by him were all things created, that are in heaven, and that are in earth, visible and invisible, whether they be thrones, or dominions, or principalities, or, powers: all things were created by him, and for him. And he is before all things, and by him all things consist. And he is the head of the body, the church: who is the beginning, the firstborn from the dead; that in all things he might have the preeminence" (Col 1:15–18). Luke said, "Neither is there salvation in any other; for there is none other name under heaven given among men, whereby we must be saved" (Acts 4:12).

Each of the beasts had six wings, and they were full of eyes. They sang night and day, singing that the Lord is Holy and that He was almighty and that He was that which was, is, and is to come. After the beast sang, then the twenty-four elders fell down or bowed down at God's feet. They worshipped him and praised him, and they even cast down their crowns before him to show reverence, servitude, and submissiveness to God their almighty.

They sang in adoration: "Thou art worthy, O Lord, to receive glory and honour and power: for thou hast created all things, and for thy pleasure they are and were created." Listen, followers of Christ. If there is anything that we can learn from these four living creatures and elders, it is to praise and worship God consistently. David said, "I will bless the Lord at all times, praise shall continually be in my mouth" (Psalm 34:1). Praising God keeps things in perspective. It reminds us that God is, and should be, the first and foremost priority of our lives. It should remind us that we are his subjects, and he is our King.

5:1–5

Chapter 5 opens up with John seeing a book in the right hand of God, while He was sitting on his throne. The book was written on both sides, and on the back of the book it contains seven seals. As I began to explain this, let me say first of all that the book that was mentioned did not look like the books of today. The book that is described in this passage of scripture is called a scroll. Books or rolls of scrolls were made of papyrus, and at the end of the scroll were wooden handles that the reader used to roll open the scroll to read them. Therefore, we can imagine that it was such a roll that was in the right hand of God. The fact that it was held by God's right hand is to show who's in control, ownership, and authority of the scroll.

As John looked at the scroll, he noticed something written on the inside as well as the outside, and that it had seven seals upon it, suggesting the profound revelation that it contained. In the ancient days, it was Roman law to seal wills with the seals of seven witnesses, with the witnesses having their own seal. At the time that the will was to be read, each witness had to remove their own seal or a delegated representative for the witness could remove it.

We can say that the scroll that God held in his hand was the last will and testament for the people who were left behind after the Rapture of the Church. Seals were also used to keep its documents a secret, as well as from people altering and tampering with the original document. John, the beloved disciple, then saw a strong angel say with a loud voice, "Who is worthy to open the book, and to loose the seals thereof?" The angel would be a mighty messenger from God. In Greek, it is pronounced *ισχυρος αγγελος*—mighty messenger.

As John waited patiently to see who would come forward, he began to cry because no one came forth—no one from heaven and no one from earth. He cried because no one was found worthy to open the book. Could it be that God's secret concerning man's judgment upon earth will stay a secret? Or could it be that God would provide a ram caught in a thicket? (See Gen. 22:8–13.)

To John's surprise, his weeping was turned into elation when he heard one of the twenty-four angels say to him, "weep not: behold, the Lion of the tribe of Judah, the root of David, hath prevailed to open the book, and to release the seven seals." The lion of the tribe of Judah and the root of David is Jesus Christ (Gen. 49:9–10; Isa. 11:1). He and only He are able to open the book and to release the seven seals.

By Jesus opening the book shows us first of all that he is a God that comes right on time. Many times, as we travel through life, Satan plays mind games of deception. He always tries to influence the people of earth that there is no hope for them. Well, my Christian friends, the devil is a liar, and the truth is not in him. He was a liar in the beginning, and he is a liar now. However, with Christ there is always hope.

He is the way, the truth, and the life. And he will always show up on time. Second, Christ is worthy to open the scrolls because he knew no sin, and neither was guile found in his mouth (2 Cor 5:21). Third, he overcame Satan's temptation, sin, and death (Matt 5:1–11; Rom 5:8, 19; 1 Cor 15:55).

5:6–10

As John watched excitedly, he saw Jesus Christ, the Lamb of God. The Greek word *lamb* in this text is the word *αρνιον/arnion*, meaning little or gentle lamb. There is no doubt that the lamb in the midst of the throne, four beasts, and elders is Christ. I like to think that the word *gentle* portrays Christ as a little and gentle lamb as one who went to the cross willingly and obediently and not one who rebelled and put up a fight to keep himself being crucified.

Yes, Christian friends, Christ was led to the slaughter as an obedient lamb to die for the sins of the world. John said, "For God so loved the world that he gave his only begotten son that whosoever believeth in him shall not perish, but have everlasting life" (John 3:16). The seven horns in this verse depict Christ's complete authority over the judgment that he is getting ready to release upon the earth. In other words, the Great Tribulation period is about to begin.

Christ then takes the book out of the right hand of God, who sat upon the throne. In the process of doing this, the elders, as well as the four beasts, began to praise God with harps. I like this verse because as they praised God, they sang with deep appreciation and summarized what Christ had done for the people of earth who trusted in him as Savior of the world. They sang, "Thou was slain and hast redeemed us by the blood." Yes, my Christian friends, there is power in the blood of the Lamb.

Not only did the twenty-four elders, as well as the four beasts, praise God but also the thousands upon thousands of angels. Wow! Talking about a mass heavenly choir that's not ashamed to worship and praise the only true and living God. Can you imagine the harmony, the unity, and the excitement that was demonstrated as they all praised God in one accord? Also, the creatures on earth, as well as under the earth joined in with the praise. There is going to come a time when all men must recognize and praise Jesus as the true Lord and Savior. (See Isa. 45:14–25, Rom 14:11; Phil 2:11.)

6:1-8

As we begin chapter 6, keep in mind that this marks the series of judgments that Christ releases upon the earth. This chapter also introduces us to the Four Horsemen of the Apocalypse. The Church is not on earth at this time, but in heaven. John witnessed Christ opening the first seal, and as he opened it, he heard a sound of thunder. This noise of thunder could be the voice of one of the four beasts that said, "Come and see." The beast invited John to come closer to witness a rider on a white horse; the rider's mission was to conquer the people of earth with malicious deception.

A bow and a crown were given to him. The bow is symbolic of military power, and the crown in this text is symbolic of conquest. Now what does all this mean? Let me first say that the person on the white horse is not Christ. Christ is the one who had just released the seal of judgment; he is in control of all things. This person is no other than the Antichrist.

The Antichrist is going to deceive the world through false peace and securities. Paul said, "For when they shall say, Peace and safety; then sudden destruction cometh upon them, as travail upon a woman with child; and they shall not escape" (1 Thess. 5:13). who is the Antichrist? We will cover more about him in chapter 13, but for right now let me say he is against everything that our Lord and Savior stands for. He is a false teacher who will be empowered by the devil. John, the beloved disciple, said of him, "Who is a liar but he that denied that Jesus is the Christ?"

He is the Antichrist, that denieth the Father and the Son (1 John 2:22). The Greek word for Antichrist is *αντιχριστος/antichristos,* meaning the adversary of the Messiah. He will come to full power during the last forty-two months, which are the last three and a half years of the Great Tribulation period. John said, "And there was given unto him a mouth speaking great things and blasphemies; and power was given unto him to continue forty and two months" (Rev. 13:5).

When Christ opened the second seal, John heard the second beast saying, "Come and see." As soon as the beast said that, John saw another horseman that was red in color and power to take away peace from the earth. This was done so that war would start on the earth. In other words, the second seal that Christ opened will be a judgment of bloodshed and rebellion.

The peace and safety plan of the Antichrist will be proven counterfeit and false and temporary. I can imagine that this day of destruction will be a day that's going to take the people of earth by surprise. Bloodshed and chaos will be the new norm. Our world today has its problems and bloodshed, but this is going to be a day and a time that the earth has never seen before. Think about it: if you can imagine a world where there is no police order, no military forces, and no fire department, and a world where everyone is against one another, then you can imagine how messed up the world can be. It's going to be a time when father is against son, daughter against mother, a time when there will be no such thing as neighborly love; this will be replaced with neighborly hate and division. I can imagine that prejudices, as well as racial injustice, will be worse than it is now. The days of helping your fellow man will be over. It's going to be a time of heartache, devastation, and pain. Nation will be against nation, and city and towns will rise against one another (Zech. 14:13; Isa. 19:2).

Jesus said, "Take heed that no man deceives you. For many shall come in my name, saying I am the Christ; and shall deceive many. And ye shall hear of wars; see that ye be not trouble: for all these things, must come to pass, but the end is not yet. For nation shall rise against nation, and kingdom against kingdom; and there shall be famine, and pestilences, and earthquakes, in diverse places, All these are the beginning of sorrow… For then shall be great tribulation, such as was not since the beginning of the world to this time, no, nor ever shall be… For there shall arise false Christ, and false prophets, and shall shew great signs and wonders; insomuch that, if it were possible, they shall deceive the very elect" (Matt. 24:4–8; 21, 24).

As John noticed Christ opening the third seal, he heard the third beast invite him to come and notice the third horseman of the apocalypse. The rider was riding on a black horse, and in his hands he had a pair of balances. John then heard a voice say, "A measure of wheat for a penny, and three measures of barley for a penny; and see thou hurt not the oil and the wine."

The denarius or penny was the average pay for a day's work. Therefore, it is implied that families would only have enough money to buy some food but nothing else. The symbolic interpretation of this black horse and the balances that he held in his hand is symbolic of harsh and severe famine in the land. Food will be scarce, and will have ridiculously high prices, to the point where some people won't be able to afford them.

The oil and the wine will not be affected as much because their roots grow deeper in the earth than the roots of corn. I feel that the word *wheat* in this text is symbolic of bread and food. In other words, the lack of food and its expensive cost will be a judgment against the people of earth; it will be the penalty for those who had not accepted Christ. They will be left behind to endure the Great Tribulation period (see Leviticus 26:26; Ezekiel 4:16).

As Christ opened the fourth seal, he noticed that the fourth rider was riding a pale horse. The word *pale* in Greek is the word χλωρος/*chloros*, meaning green or yellowish pale. It is implied that the fourth horseman's face is going to be bleached or saturated with terror to the point that his complexion is going to mirror the doom and plight of his victims.

The name of the fourth rider is called death, and he is followed by hell. The word *hell* in this text can be a metaphor to imply the suffering and destruction that he will bring with him to the disobedient people of earth. Power was given to him to kill a quarter part of earth's population with sickness and disease. The Greek word for *death* is the word θανατος/*thanatos* meaning death, but in this text not only does it mean death, but it also means pestilence.

Webster's Dictionary defines pestilence as "a contagious or infectious epidemic that is virulent and devastating: Bubonic Plague; something that is destructive or pernicious." Therefore, as the fourth rider goes forth upon the earth, he will be releasing woes of infectious diseases that will bring about millions of fatalities. Personally, it is my opinion that these destructive and deadly viruses will be airborne, quickly devouring the population of the earth.

I also feel that some of the old, deadly viruses will return but more deadly than ever before. It is also my opinion that new plagues will come into existence that will be deadlier than the Black Death that killed off more than seventy-five to two hundred million people in Europe during the Middle Ages (1346–1353).

Not only will there be deadly pandemic diseases, but food will be scarce, wars will be fought, and also certain animals will turn against man and devour them. Think about it, friends, not only will mankind be hungry during these times, but wild and beastly animals as well.

Notice what Ezekiel said, "For thus saith the Lord God; How much more when I send my four sore judgments upon Jerusalem, the sword, and the famine, and the noisome beast, and the pestilence, to cut off from it man and beast" (Ezek. 14:21). Moses said in the Book of Leviticus, "I will bring seven times more plagues among you according to your sins... I will send wild beasts among you, which shall rob you of your children, and destroy your cattle... I will bring a sword upon you...ye shall eat and not be satisfied" (Leviticus 26:21–26).

Listen, coworkers of Christ, it's going to be a terrible time during the Great Tribulation period, because when Christ opened the fourth seal, one-fourth of the population of the world will die.

6:9–11

When Christ opened the fifth seal, John heard and noticed souls that were beneath the altar in heaven. He noticed that these souls looked like they had been slain. The Greek word for *slain* is the word σφαζω/*spahzo*, meaning to butcher, to slaughter, or to put to a violent death. These martyrs had been put to death because of their faith and testimony of God (Matt. 24:9).

But what is so significant about the altar that they were under? Well, throughout the Old and New Testament, altars were a place where sacrifices were made unto God. Blood was shed and sprinkled at the foot of the altar of the temple. Blood was regarded as the life source and showed that all life belongs to God. Moses said, "The life of all flesh is the blood" (Lev. 17: 11–14). After the priest would sacrifice the bull, they would then pour the blood at the base of the altar to show that the sacrifice was made as an offering unto the Lord (Lev. 4:7).

This explains why the souls were beneath the altar in heaven; they were there to show that the lives that were sacrificed were an offering unto the Lord. Who were these martyrs? I believe that the scripture teaches that two group of martyred saints will be present under the altar of God.

First, the scripture teaches us that these saints were Old Testament believers who will not be resurrected until the tribulation period is over. Luke said, "That the blood of all the prophets, which was shed from the foundation of the world, maybe required of this generation; from the blood of Abel unto the blood of Zacharias, which perished between the altar and the temple: verily I say unto you, it shall be require of this generation" (Luke 11:50–51).

The second group of people under the altar in heaven will be tribulation saints. The tribulation saints are people who were left behind after the Rapture of the church and have come into the saving knowledge of Jesus Christ and are killed for their profession of faith in Christ. John said, "And I saw thrones, and they sat upon them, and judgment was given unto them that were beheaded for the witness of Jesus, and for the Word of God, and which had not worshipped the beast, neither his image, neither had received his mark upon their foreheads, or in their hands; and they lived and reigned with Christ a thousand years. But the rest of the dead lived not again until the thousand years were finished. This is the first resurrection. Blessed and holy is he that hath part in the first resurrection: on such the second death hath no power, but they shall be priests of God and of Christ, and shall reign with him a thousand years" (Rev. 20:4–6).

We know that the souls underneath the altar are saved souls because of the three words that they used to depict that they have a relationship with Christ.

First, they used the word *Lord*. The word *Lord* in Greek is the word δεσποτης/*despotes* or κυριος/*kurios*, meaning Lord or master. When one becomes a believer in Christ, Christ becomes their Lord and master of their life and soul. Believers obey Christ like slaves obey their masters (Matt. 24:46).

Second, they used the word *holy*. The Greek word for *holy* is the word 'αγιος/*hagios* meaning *saint, holy one*, or "to be different." As believers of Christ, the scriptures teach us to be holy like Christ (1 Peter 1:16). Third, the souls underneath the altar used the word *true*. The Greek word for *true* is the word αληθινο/*alsthinos*, meaning "that which is real in nature; to be genuine." God is the only living and true God. He is real and genuine in every sense of the word (John 14:6; 2 Cor 1:18a; John 1:9; 1 John 5:20).

When the martyrs asked the Lord how long they would have to wait until he avenged them of their death, the Lord responded and said that they would have to wait a little while longer until their fellow believers would be killed as well. This way, all of them would be resurrected unto life of eternal victory and reward at the same time. In other words, the Old Testaments saints, as well as the tribulation saints, will be resurrected during the second resurrection.

6:12-17

As Christ opens the sixth seal, it starts the second half of the last three-and-a-half years of the tribulation period. It begins with a chain of natural and cosmic upheavals that will take place. John heard and saw a great earthquake that devastated the earth. All through the history of the world, we have heard of the countless earthquakes that have occurred upon the earth, but the earthquake that is mentioned in this text will be the most horrific earthquake of them all. He noticed that the sun that the once shone brightly will turn black, meaning it will set and turn dark earlier than before.

The moon will be the color of red, instead of the glimmering white. The stars that once stood at attention like soldiers waiting for a command fell down to the earth like figs falling from a fig tree. These devastating events were so powerful and dreadful that mountains and islands were moved and reshaped.

No one on earth could stop or run from this catastrophic storm of woes. The wealthy couldn't pay for solace, and the less fortunate couldn't find adequate shelter to protect them from this great and terrible day. It will be so terrible that there will be various earthquakes. The prophet Joel said, "The earth will shake before them; the heavens shall tremble: the sun and the moon shall be dark, and the stars shall withdraw their shining" (Joel 2:10). Even the seas, the oceans, and the lakes will be affected. Haggai the prophet declared, "For thus saith the Lord of host; Yet once, it is a little while, and I will shake the heavens, and the earth, and the sea, and the dry land" (Hag. 2:6). Again, the devastation of natural occurrences that happened when Christ opened the sixth seal caused massive earthquakes that shook the foundations of earth. It no doubt caused volcanic eruptions to release its fiery lava. One can only imagine how the explosive strength from the erupting volcanos gave way to hot ash that covered the sun. Then too the height of the ash went so far out into the atmosphere that it affected the sight of the moon and stars at night.

The shaking of the earth, or earthquakes, was so powerful that it no doubt caused many tsunamis that caused flooding on the earth. Jesus said, "And there shall be signs in the sun, and in the moon, and in the stars; and upon the earth distress of nations, with perplexity; the sea and the waves roaring; Men's hearts failing them for fear, and for looking after those things which are coming on the earth: for the powers of heaven shall be shaken" (Luke 21:25–26).

In other words, sinners who are left behind after the Rapture of the church will experience sufferings as they never suffered before. Verse 17 says, "For the great day of his wrath is come; and who shall be able to stand." This is to say that God's judgment will be against all who have not accepted him as Lord and Savior before the Church age. This analogy will also be upon those unbelievers living during the tribulation period. If they still rebelled and refused to accept Christ as Lord, then they will be doomed and feel God's wrath. It will not matter if one is rich or poor; God's wrath will be upon him. It will not matter if one country along with their military power is greater or mightier than the next. They will not stand against the wrath of God. When this great and terrible day occurs, everybody will be on the same level: all will seek refuge; all will seek to hide from God like Adam and Eve, who hid from God because of their disobedience (Gen. 3:9).

Yes, during the tribulation period, God's wrath will seek sinners out, and his justice will judge them and send them to a lake that burns with fire and brimstone. This judgment will take place after the tribulation period and millenium (Rev. 20:15).

Rev. 7:1-8

After these things, John saw four angels standing at the four corners of the earth. These corners will be the north, south, east, and west. As he saw them standing there, he saw that they were in charge of the winds. They were commanded to hold the winds and prevent them from blowing on the earth. The Psalmist tells us in Ps 148:8 that God will use the winds of the earth for judgment to carry out his will. As John continued to observe, he saw another angel coming from the east with the seal of God in his hand, and he cried out to the other angels and instructed them by saying hurt not the earth, seas, and the trees until the servants of God be sealed in their foreheads.

The angel that is mentioned in this text is the fifth angel of the apocalypse, and he outranks the four other angels. I say this because John observed him instructing the other angel by the authority of his loud voice. The Greek words for "loud voice" are the words *μεγας/megale φωνη/phone*; it is where we get our English word *megaphone*. Therefore, it is with a great and loud voice of authority that this fifth angel commands the four other angels. Those servants of God that were sealed were 144 thousand Jews from the tribes of Israel, as well as countless Gentiles who were saved during the tribulation period.

Again, he tells the four angels to hold back the winds of judgment until God's servants on earth be sealed. (Read Ezekiel 9:1–7.)

I do not know what type of seal this will be. However, the seal will help them go through and endure the second half of the tribulation period. Jesus said, "For then shall be great tribulation, such as was not since the beginning of the world to this time, no, nor ever shall be. And except those days should be shortened, there should no flesh be saved: but for the elect sake those days shall be shortened" (Matthew 24:21–2).

If Satan can seal his people and only allow those who are sealed with the mark of the beast to buy and sell, God can certainly seal the people that belong to him from the worst wrath that has ever come upon man.

These beginning verses of chapter 7 also shows us the matchless grace and love of God. The thought of God giving the lost another chance to accept Christ after the Rapture of the church is love at its best. No wonder Peter said, "The Lord is not slack concerning his promise, as some men count slackness; but is longsuffering to us-ward, not willing that any should perish, but that all should come to repentance" (2 Pe 3:9). But how can these people get saved now that the ministry of the church is over? Good question. God is going to use the 144 thousand Jews to preach and be a witness for Christ (Matt 24:14).

He is also going to use the two witnesses to preach and be a witness for him (Rev. 11:3). God is also going to use the ministry of the Holy Spirit to influence, to convict of sin, and to bear witness of the truth. Notice again that the 144 thousand are made up of Jews, twelve thousand from each tribe. However, the tribe of Dan and Ephraim are not listed because they fell into idolatry (Jud. 18:30; Hos. 4:17). Ephraim was also the tribe that led in the division of the kingdom (1 Ki. 11:26). Joseph takes the place of Ephraim on the list, and Levi takes the place of the tribe of Dan. Point to ponder: don't allow sin to make you lose your position in God.

7:9-17

After John saw the 144,000, he saw an endless number that no man can count standing before the throne of God. One of the elders asked John, did he know who these people were who were dressed in white? John replied, "Sir, you know."

The elder then responded and said, "These are they who have come out of the great tribulation. They have washed their robes and made them white in the blood of the lamb."

The number of people was so great that it were beyond the ability of one man to count them. Their apparel was made white to symbolize that they were martyred for the faithful testimony of Christ; they were killed because they refused to succumb to the wicked side of the Antichrist. But nevertheless, them washing their robes in the blood of the lamb was also to show that the blood of Christ and what it represented made them overcomers; for truly they were now eternally safe in the presence of the Lord.

After the tribulation saints praised God, the angels stood around God's throne and around the elders and four beasts, and as they bowed down before God Christ, they sang with jubilation and said, "Amen: blessings and glory, and wisdom, and thanksgiving, and honor, and power, and might be unto our God, forever and ever. Amen."

Their faith in Christ was so committed and loyal that they died for their faith in the Savior. The tribulation saints were so elated about their religious triumph that to show their appreciation for their salvation and victory, they served Christ day and night in his temple. Let me stick a pin here and say that acts of gratitude should be done toward Christ for the things that he has done for our lives.

I believe when we as believers of Christ worship him day and night, blessings will follow. The elder told John that the tribulation saints will never have to worry about eating; they would never have to worry about being thirsty. Why? Christ our Savior will see to their needs.

The tears that they shed would no longer be a symbol of pain and suffering; they would be replaced by tears of joy. In other words, God will give them comfort and joy while, at the same time, he would wipe the tears from their weeping eyes.

Beloved, we serve a God of might and joy. He knows how to be a God of strength and comfort. Jeremiah said, "Then shall the virgins rejoice in the dance, both young men and old together: for I will turn their morning into joy, and will comfort them, and make them rejoice from their sorrow. And I will satiate the souls of the priest with fatness, and my people shall be satisfied with my goodness, saith the Lord" (Jer. 31:13–14).

8:1–13

As we read in chapter 8, John noticed Christ as he opened the 7th seal. There was silence in heaven for a period of a half hour. You may ask: why was there silence in heaven when Christ opened the seventh seal? What was so important that all heaven ceases it jubilant praise? Or what was so important to Christ that he stopped and paused from his work of judgment that he allowed an interlude of calmness to occur for half an hour?

I purpose two speculative theories of interpretation. It is said that before each storm there is a quiet calmness. If that old wives' tale be true, this half an hour of silence that was mentioned when Christ opened the seventh seal set the stage for an oncoming storm of judgment that was about to hit the earth. God works in mysterious and strange ways, but no matter how he chooses to work, it is to get our attention.

When there is an eerie calm before a great storm, man takes notice that something is going to happen. The prophet Isaiah said, "For the Lord shall rise up as in mount Perazim, he shall be wroth; and bring to pass his act, his strange act" (Isa. 28:21). Second, the silence in heaven could be taken as Christ being so interested in hearing the prayers of the saints that he quiets heaven and focuses all of his attention to hear and receive their prayers. The Psalmist said,

"The eyes of the Lord are upon the righteous, and his ears are open unto their cry" (Ps. 34:15).

John then saw seven angels standing around God's throne, and they were given seven trumpets. John also saw another angel standing at the altar, and in his hand was a golden censer. He was given much incense to offer at the altar, along with the prayers of the saints.

These seven angels were special angels that stood in the presence of God, waiting for his commands for instruction of service. It was the angel Gabriel who received instructions from the Lord to announce the birth of John the Baptist to Zacharias. He said, "I am Gabriel that stand in the presence of God" (Luke 1:10).

Another group of angels who stand in the presence of God is the seraphim, but they have a different mission from the other group of angels that is mentioned in Revelation 8:2. These angels used their trumpets to announce an event of God's intervention. Zephaniah said, "A day of the trumpet and alarm against the fenced cities, and against the high towers, and I will bring distress upon men, that they shall walk like blind men, because they have sinned against the Lord: and their blood shall be poured out as dust, and their flesh as the dung (Zep. 1:16–17).

As the angel offered the incense along with the prayers of the saints, it ascended up to God like smoke that rises to the sky. As the incense as well as the prayers rose up before God, the angel took that same censer and filled it with the fire from the altar of God and cast it down into the earth, causing natural and atmospheric happenings and devastation on the earth.

The devastation to the earth that was caused by the angel are as follows: When the first angel blew his trumpet of judgment, it was followed by a mixture of hail, fire, and blood. It appears to me that these three elements were a blend/medley of all three together and not independent from each other because the KJV uses the word mingle, which is μίγνυμι/ *mignumi*, which in the Greek means to mix or to mingle. Friends, I'm neither a scientist nor a physicist, but ice melts when fire is put to it. This is to say and to prove that the God that we serve is all powerful. He is in control of all things; he is the maker and creator of ice, fire, and blood, so certainly he can tell them what to do as well as how to cooperate with one another.

Think about it. He created the heaven and the earth by simply saying, "Let there be…" He made Adam from dirt/dust, he turned water into wine, he walked on water, and even brought back the dead. God can do anything. There is no limit to his power. Then too the mixture of hail, fire, and blood could be a shower of small meteors plunging down to earth. I have even heard some say that this can be interpreted as launched missiles. No matter what interpretation side you are on, it is Christ who is behind all judgments during this time. When the destructive element hit the earth, it burned a third part of the trees and grass. My wife and I do a lot of camping in state parks, and we have really noticed and enjoyed the beauty of God's nature as we walked the scenic trails. I can only imagine how terrible it will look if it was burned up.

When the second angel blew his horn, there appeared to be something as large as a burning mountain that was cast into the sea. This large burning object could be a falling meteor that splashed into the sea, destroying a third part of all living sea creatures. The many ships upon the water were destroyed as well. When the third angel blew his trumpet, John sees a star that is falling out of the sky. Once again, this can be interpreted as a meteor of colossal size that destroyed a third part of the rivers as well as the fountain of waters. The star was called wormwood; in the Greek, it is the word ἄψινθος/ *ápsinthos,* and it means bitterness, poisonous, and calamity.

The earth's waters will be unfit to drink, and many people will die because of it. Based upon the last three trumpets of judgment, it would appear that the water supply of the earth will be affected. Can you imagine the agony of the tribulation age people when they find out that they have no good water to drink? Think about it. It is said that 71 percent of the earth's surface is covered by water, and this does not include the oceans. So when you talk about a third part of the seas and rivers and various waters, you're talking about a great number of waters that will be made bitter. When the fourth angel sounded his trumpet, the third part of the sun, the moon, and the stars were covered with darkness. When that happens, the days and evenings will be short as well.

Think of it this way. When a third part of the sun gets covered with darkness, it will affect solar power, crops, and even the earth's climate will change. I can even imagine the moods or mindsets of the tribulation inhabitants will change for the worse. We need the sunlight; it's good for our physical and mental well-being. As the third part of darkness continues, an angel flew through the sky and said with a loud voice, "Woe, woe, woe to the inhabitants the of earth." The angel said this because more judgments were coming.

9:1-12

After John witnessed the natural devastation that were brought on by the four angels that blew their trumpets, he then noticed, as a seer, a fifth angel blowing his trumpet. As he blew it, a star fell from heaven to the earth. The star was given a key to the bottomless pit. As he opened it, he saw that the smoke from the pit was so dark and in abundance that it covered the sun and filled the air. While the smoke ascended, out from the long-shafted pit came what appeared to be locusts upon the earth, and they were given power like unto scorpions. It is my belief that the star that fell from heaven is not symbolic of a meteor that we saw in chapter 8:10–11; this star is symbolic of Satan himself. I say this because Isaiah the prophet said of Satan, "How art thou fallen from heaven, O Lucifer, son of the morning!" (Isa. 14:12). Then too, Jesus said, "And he said unto, them, I beheld Satan as lighting fall from heaven" (Luke 10:18).

The apostle Paul also writes: "And no marvel; for Satan, himself is transformed into an angel of light" (2 Cor 11:14).

The locusts that John saw are to be taken as a plague of demons released by Satan to cause torment and suffering of the worst kind upon those people who have not the seal of God upon their foreheads. Their woes are to be compared to the sting of a scorpion tail, which causes severe pain and agony from its poison. Plagues of locusts were also used as judgment against Pharaoh and his Egyptian empire for refusing to let God's people go (Ex.10:1–20).

But unlike those locusts that attacked Egypt's vegetation, these plagues of demons were given orders not to hurt the earth, but to torment the evil people of earth for a period of five months. These people were going to be in so much pain that they would wish that they would die, but they would not die; death would not be a remedy for their misery. Even suicide in its worst imaginable way will not be possible. Notice the shape of these locusts. John said that they were as tall as horses, and they were organized for battle. On the top of their heads were crowns of gold, and their face resembled the face of a man. They had long hair and the teeth of a ferocious lion. Each locust had on breastplates of iron, and their wings sounded like many chariots moving into battle. (See Joel 2:1–11.)

These descriptions allow us to know that they were to be feared and that they were prepared like armored soldiers who were ready to claim victory on their oncoming war. The demon locusts had a king over them, meaning they were under his authority, and they were his demonic subjects. The king's name was *Abaddon* in the Hebrew language, and it means destruction; he is also the angel of the infernal region. His name also means, in Hebrew, the minister of death and the author of havoc on the earth. His name in Greek is *Apollum*, meaning the destroyer.

9:13–21

When the sixth angel blew his trumpet, John heard a voice coming from the four horns of the golden altar. The altar is symbolic of prayer that goes up before the presence of God. I know this because when Christ opened the seventh seal in the beginning of chapter 8, seven angels stood in the presence of God, and another angel stood before him with incense to offer the prayers of the saints upon the golden altar (8:3).

It was symbolic of prayer because the altar was used by the priest in the Old Testament to burn incense unto God. It was also used once a year on the Day of Atonement.

When the four angels were released, they had power to kill a third of the earth's population.

When the fifth angel blew his trumpet, the demonic locusts were not allowed to kill the people; they were allowed to inflict severe pain and sufferings to their lives. But now we see the sixth angel releasing four evil angels upon earth to kill a third of the human race.

Some compare this army to that of the Parthian Empire, who was the Roman Empire's archenemy. They dwelled near the Euphrates River and were known for their boldness in battle. They could not be trusted, they were also skilled in archery; they had the ability of sitting backward on their horses, and while their horses moved forward, they would shoot their arrows at their enemies.

John describes the armored breastplate as fiery red, jacinth, and smoky blue bordering the color black. It was also the color of sulfurous yellow, the color of hot brimstone. These colors depict colors of a glowing flame of fire. This is to say that this army will be hot with the rage of vengeance, consuming everything within their path like wild fire. Their horses' heads are described to resemble the heads of lions, and their tail is likened to the tails of serpents. This is to say that their army will invoke fear and intimidation, and they will move like serpents, devouring their prey with cunning, warlike maneuvers.

You would think that through all of this death and destruction that those who were left alive would repent from their sins of idolatry and confess faith in Christ, but they did not; they still allowed evil to consume them, and they continued wholeheartedly in their sins of wickedness. They willingly continued in their sins of idolatry.

The Greek word for *idols* is the word ειδωλον/*eidolon*, meaning an image or likeness for worship—a false god. John also said they refused to repent of their fornication. The Greek word for *fornication* is the word πορνεια/*porneia*, meaning illicit sexual intercourse, homosexuality, lesbianism, intercourse with animals, sexual intercourse with close relatives, and sexual intercourse with a divorced man or woman (Mark 10:11–12).

They continued in theft. The Greek word for *theft* is the word κλεμμα/*klemma*, which means "a thing stolen or the act of theft." They continued in murder. The Greek word for *murder* is the word φονος/*phonos*, meaning to slaughter or to be slain. They continued in sorceries. The Greek word for *sorceries* is the word φαρμακεια/

pharmakeia, which means *sorcery*, *witchcraft*, "to use or the administering of drugs," *magical arts*, and "the deceptions and seduction of idolatry."

They continued in devil worship. The Greek word for *devil* is the word δαιμονιον/*daimonion*, meaning a devil, a spirit inferior to God, evil spirits, or the messengers and ministers of the devil. Solomon said, "There is a way that seemeth right unto man, but the end thereof are the ways to death" (Proverbs 16:25).

10:1-4

As we approach chapter 10s and 11, there is another interlude or break between the sixth and the seventh trumpets. As you recall, there was an interlude between the sixth and seventh seal so that the people of God can be sealed. However, in this chapter, three personalities will be revealed. They are the mighty angel, who may or may not be Christ, and the two witnesses that may be two of the following people: Moses, Elijah, or Enoch. John, the seer and revelator, said he saw a mighty angel that came down from heaven.

He was clothed in a cloud, and on his head was a rainbow. His face was, as it were, the sun; and his feet were, as it was, pillars of fire. Who was this angel? The angel that is described is just a mighty angel; he is not Christ.

Christ is the one bringing about judgment upon people left behind after the Rapture.

Christ will not come down out of heaven to actually touch earth until the millennium. This is when he establishes his kingdom upon earth for a thousand years, and when he finally destroys wickedness to judge the sinners at the Great White Throne Judgment. He will also cast Satan into the lake of fire and then usher his people into the eternal state with him. We will cover this more in detail a little bit later. But for right now, I feel that the mighty angel described here is not Christ. However, you are welcome to disagree. The mighty angel was also clothed in a cloud, and a rainbow was upon his head and his feet, was as a pillar of fire. First of all, the angel clothed in a cloud is to be interpreted as a means of transport mobility. The Psalmist said, "Who maketh the cloud his chariot" (Psalm 104:3).

The rainbow upon his head is probably a reminder to the earth that God is to still fulfill his promise that the earth will not be destroyed by water anymore (Gen. 9:8–17). His face shone as the sun to depict that he was around the throne and presence of God. Moses's face shone when he was in the presence of God (Exod. 34:35).

The angel's feet were like pillars of fire. This is to say that the angel was part of God's judgment, that he was going to purify the earth from its evil and wickedness. His voice was the voice of a lion. The lion's roar is loud and intimidating; it gets the attention of the hearer and sets the stage of fear and on coming doom. The angel put his right foot on the sea and his left foot on the earth. He also had in his hand an open book.

When the angel cried out, John heard seven thunderous voices. What was this book, and what did the thunderous voices represent? The book is the seven-seal book that no one was able to open but Christ. God the Father gave it to him (5:1–7); Christ gave it to the mighty angel, and then the mighty angel gave it to John the revelator to eat. When the mighty angel places his feet on the land and sea, it is to show that God owns the earth (Ps. 8:6–8; 24:1).

The loud, thunderous voices are the voice of God agreeing to what is about to happen; it's as if God himself is saying, Amen (or so be it). However, the thunderous voice of God said more than this. Whatever was said, John was instructed not to write it. Why did God tell John not to write down what was said? No one knows. Many people have speculated, but no one knows for sure. Me and Deacon Orr—who was a faithful deacon of the church that I pastored—he and I, when it comes to a time when we cannot explain scripture soundly and with the upmost honesty, we jokingly quote without hesitation in our eyes as the eleventh commandment, and that is, "That the secret things belongs to the Lord" (Deut 29:29).

The mighty angel then lifted his hands toward heaven and swore that the time of man's delay is over. No longer would the unjust continue doing wicked and evil things and get away with them; no longer would an unrighteous government justify its actions. It was time for the final seal to be released and judgment of the worst kind to occur.

When the seventh angel blew the seventh trumpet, the mystery of God would be revealed and finished. This is to say that all unanswered questions about man in God's eternal plan will be answered.

John taking and eating the book is to show first of all that it has a sweetness affect to the point of knowing that Lord Jesus is in control of all things and that he will reign victoriously over evil and over the wickedness of man. Sweetness brings about joy and gladness to the senses. Therefore, it is joy and gladness that the child of God finds when they know that Christ is the orchestrator of all things, and it is with that faith that brings gladness to their soul. However, the bitterness is the judgments that the unsaved will feel when they face Christ's wrath.

11:1-14

A measuring reed was given to John to measure God's temple. Reeds were stalks of grass that grew like bamboo canes, which grew to heights of six to nine feet high. They would cut the poles or rods into a Jewish unit of measurement and call them cubits. Therefore, a normal length of a measuring rod was about six cubits, which is about seventeen to eighteen inches.

The cubit was originally the space from the tip of the middle finger to the edge of the elbow. These poles were use as measuring sticks. Rods were not only used for measuring sticks, but shepherds also used them to fend off wild animals like wolves from their sheep. When David said, "Thy rod and the staff comfort me," it is to show that God protects him from his enemies, like shepherds protect their sheep, and because he is protected, he is comforted.

The idea of measuring is not something that the scriptures are foreign to; it was commonly used out through the Old Testament. We find it in Eze. 40:3, 6; Zach. 2:1; and Amos 7:7–9. Therefore, I'm quite sure that John the revelator had these scriptures in mind when he was given a rod to measure the temple.

Notice, John said that their destruction would be forty-two months, which is three and half years, which is the second half of the tribulation period. In others words, for ungodly men as well as the Antichrist, wickedness would only last for another three and a half years before Christ comes back to establish his millennium kingdom upon earth.

During that time, Christ will give power to two of his witnesses. Their main objective is to get people to repent from their sins and to accept Christ as Savior. No one knows for sure who these two witnesses will be.

Some say that they will be two of the following three: Moses, Enoch, and Elijah. Some even believe that it will be none of the three that were just mentioned, but that they will be two of the ones that were sealed during the tribulation period and that they would be chosen to do great miracles for God.

Some say that the two witnesses will testify concerning Christ during the first half of the tribulation period, and some say they will be given power to testify of Christ during the last part of the tribulation period. However, I feel that their supernatural ministry will take place during the first half of the tribulation period, because they kept doing the works of God until the Antichrist appeared on the scene, and then they were killed. They were noted as being the two olive trees and lampstands that would stand for God in the midst of the tribulation period on earth.

In the Old Testament, the olive trees and lampstands were that of Joshua and Zerubbabel, who were empowered by the Holy Ghost to stand against the attacks against God's people during that time period (Zech. 4:3, 11). The two witnesses are going to be so empowered by the Holy Spirit that they will be immune to satanic attacks until their mission is over.

To show the hatred and cruelty during that time of the tribulation period, the two witnesses were not even given a decent burial. They were left out in the streets to vex the other believers and to make them out of a public spectacle. Matter of fact, they were left in the streets for a period of three days and a half, for the people of all nations to gaze upon them with mockery.

The ungodly will be so happy that these men are dead, that they will be celebrating like it's Christmas—meaning that they would be exchanging gifts to one another to celebrate the two witnesses' death. Jerusalem is the great city that is referred to in verse 8. However, because of the wickedness of that time, it will be compared to Sodom and Egypt

After the three and a half days is over, the two witnesses will come back to life and stand on their feet. Just like God, when he breathed into man and man became a living soul. God will put life back into the dead bodies of the witnesses and restore them back to life. Can you imagine how the ungodly will feel when they see these witnesses coming back to life?

In the midst of their rejoicing and in the midst of their temporary victory, the bodies that they were rejoicing over or even danced over were brought back to life. I wonder if their facial expression gave them a glimpse of their coming and impending doom. When they stood on their feet, they heard a voice from heaven saying unto them, "Come up hither." Let me stick a pen here and say that the act of them standing and hearing validates and proves that they were really alive; for the dead can't stand on their own, nor can the dead hear. During the same hour, when the two witnesses went up to heaven, an earthquake devastated the city of Jerusalem and killed seven thousand people. The remnant that was left over gave God the glory, but the glory that they gave to God was more so out of fear and not of faith.

11:15-19

As the two witnesses were caught up to heaven, John noticed that the seventh angel was prepared to sound his trumpet. However, the sounding of the trumpet was not immediate. When it does sound, it will lead us into the millennium. The second woe has just ended, and the third woe of judgments is about to happen briefly. Remember, woes are destruction of judgments that are carried out upon the evil men on earth. To magnify the agony of the wicked, the Greek word for woe is **οὐαί /ouaí,** meaning grief and misery.

Yes, because of God's judgment upon the wicked unbelievers, grief and misery will accompany their everyday life. It will be likened to their own dark shadows; no matter where they go or how fast they run, misery will follow them. Each woe is more devastating than the previous.

Six trumpet judgments, including two woes, are concluded; fear awaits them, as they look toward the future with oncoming gloom and despair. When the seventh trumpet did sound, John heard voices in heaven announcing that the kingdom of this world had become the kingdom of our Lord Jesus Christ. No longer would the devil be known as the father of this world. No longer would this world be governed by sin, wickedness, and unfairness. Christ would soon be the long and expected Messiah of the world. When the twenty-four elders heard this proclamation, they fell down prostrate to worship God. They said with jubilant voices, "We give thee thanks, o Lord God almighty, which art, and wast, and art to come; because thou hast taken to thee thy great power, and hast reigned."

When Christ returns, many will be elated at his arrival. However, those who had rejected him will be saddened at the coming of his Kingdom (11:16–17; 20:7–15).

Verse 19 tells us that the temple of God was opened in heaven. This is to be taken that no one would be barred from worshipping God. Access to God for the purpose of worship would be granted and open to all, for all, with emphasis on Israel.

The words "And the ark of his covenant was seen in his sanctuary," these words are to remind Israel that he is still a covenant keeping God, and he will keep his promise to his people. Jeremiah said, "Behold, the days come, saith the Lord, that I will make a new covenant with the house of Israel, and with the house of Judah: Not according to the covenant that I made with their fathers in the day that I took them by the hand to bring them out of the land of Egypt; which my covenant they brake, although I was a husband unto them, saith the Lord: But this shall be the covenant that I will make with the house of Israel; After those days, saith the Lord, I will put my law in the inward parts, and write it in their heart; and will be their God, and they shall be my people. And they shall teach no more every man his neighbor, and every man his brother, saying, know the lord: for they shall all know me, from the least of them to the greatest of them, saith the Lord: for I will forgive their iniquity, and I will remember their sin no more" (Jeremiah 31:31–34).

The words: lightning, voices and earthquakes sets the stage for more oncoming judgements that will happen to the people of the earth.

12:1–6

As we open the door to chapter 12, John the beloved disciple saw a great wonder in heaven. The Greek word for *wonder* is the word σημειον/*semeion*, meaning *sign, miracle*, or "an unusual occurrence, transcending the common course of nature."

In other words, John saw within a vision a supernatural sign, a wonder in heaven that describes the nation of Israel. Why Israel? Well, back in the Old Testament, there was a young man named Joseph, who dreamed a dream. Moses said, "And he dreamed yet another dream, and told it to his brethren, and said, Behold, I have dreamed a dream more; and behold, the sun and the moon and the eleven stars made obeisance to me. And he told it to his father, and to his brethren; and his father rebukes him, and said unto him, what is this dream that thou hast dreamed? Shall I and thy mother and thy brethren indeed come to bow down ourselves to thee to the earth?" (Gen. 37:9–10).

I agree with the mindset of Jacob, because his name was changed to Israel. Therefore he, Jacob, represented Israel as a nation. And since he is Israel, it is to say that Israel is identified as the woman that gave birth to a child. The child is the Messiah; Jesus Christ was born through the nation of Israel.

John the revelator saw another sign in heaven. He saw a red dragon with seven heads and ten horns; there were also seven crowns upon his heads. His tail influenced a third part of the stars of heaven, and he along with the stars was cast down to the earth. The dragon stood waiting to devour the woman as soon as she would give birth to her child. What does all this mean and who is the dragon?

The red dragon is symbolic of Satan. He is called great because of his great destructive power of evil. He is red in color to depict the malevolent bloodshed that he will cause during the Great Tribulation period. Matter of fact, he is called a murderer from the beginning (John 8:44). He is called a dragon because a dragon has four wings for speed and a body like a serpent to show that he will deceive the world with craftiness and poisonous hatred. In some cases, dragons are known to breath out fire.

This is to say that Satan's words are not to be trusted. He is the father of all liars. His words may seem warm and enticing, but once you get within the range of his fire, he will burn you from all hopes and dreams. Jesus said, "The thief cometh not but for to steal, and to kill, and to destroy: I am come that they might have life, and that they might have it more abundantly" (John 10:10).

The seven heads are a symbol of wisdom, and the number seven represents fullness and completeness. Also, the dragon having seven heads and ten horns is to say that Satan will be in authority over seven nations. He will start out with ten, to show reference to the ten horns, but he will overtake or subdue three of them (17:12, Dan. 7:7–8; 20, 24; Rev. 13:1). Satan has always used his cunning wisdom to deceive the world. (Isa. 14:16–17).

God said, "And I will put enmity between thee and the woman, and between thy seed and her seed; it shall bruise thy head and thou shalt bruise his heel" (Gen. 3:15).

This is to say that a time is going to come when Christ will destroy the head of the serpent, as well as his demonic kingdom. Even though Satan will bruise the heel of Christ—his crucifixion—Christ in turn will defeat him by his atoning death, his resurrection, and also by casting the devil and his false prophets into hell. Notice what John the beloved disciple said, "And the devil that deceived them was cast into the lake of fire and brimstone, where the false prophet are, and shall be tormented day and night forever and ever (Rev. 20:10).

12:7-17

Verses 7 to 9 tell of an angelic war in heaven. Michael and his angels fought against the devil and his angels. However, the devil and his angels lost the war, along with their heavenly positions. Satan, along with his rebellious angels, was cast out of heaven down to earth. Let us go back and look at the word *war*; in Greek it is the word πολεμος/*polemos*, meaning *war, battle, strife, dispute,* or quarrel. Let me say that everywhere Satan goes, he always stirs up confusion and disputes. Peter said, "Be sober, be vigilant; because your adversary the devil, as a roaring lion, walketh about, seeking whom he may devour" (1 Peter 5:8).

The archangel Michael's name means "who is like God?" The meaning of Michael's name put God in a special and unique category of his own; for truly there is no other god like the God Jehovah. He is the true God, He is the creator, and He is the existing one who declared to Moses that "I am that I am," He is what He is. He is the "I am God." Jesus said, "He that hath received his testimony hath set to his seal that God is true" (John 3:33).

Yes. There is no god like Jehovah. He is in a league of his own. Even though Satan still has access to heaven even now, there is going to come a time when he will be thrown out again. Never returning to gain access (20:11; Job 1–2; Dan. 2:35; Zech. 10:10).

John, the beloved disciple, then heard a loud voice from heaven, saying, "Now is come salvation and strength and the kingdom of our God, and the power of his Christ: for the accuser of our brethren is cast down, which accused them before our God day and night." No one knows for sure who the voice was behind this praise of jubilation.

Some have said that it was the tribulation saints (Rev. 6:10, 10). But whoever he or they were, praise was directed to God for the expulsion of the devil from heaven. Victory through the manifestation of God's power had finally come to end Satan's reign and usher in the millennium kingdom, as well as the oncoming eternal state with God (cf. 11:15; Psalm 2:8).

12:13-17

When the dragon (Satan) saw that he was powerless against Christ and that he was cast down to the earth, he went to persecute or attack Israel, which I believe is the woman. The words "the woman was given two wings" is to be taken as a symbol of speed and strength. In the book of Exodus, God tells Israel how he borne them on eagles' wings and had brought them into the wilderness from the hostile Egyptians. God would do the same thing to protect them from the persecution of Satan.

The words "She is nourished for a time" may be interpreted as other nations, who are on the side of Israel, who comes to help her and protect her in her time of need. Just like there are going to be nations that will come to Israel's aid, there are going to be nations that will be against Israel as well. They will come upon Israel like a mighty flood of water. But nevertheless, the opposing nations that will be motivated by the serpent (devil) will be defeated. They will let them go after the saved remnants of Jerusalem.

13:1-10

As we begin to study chapter 13, let's keep in mind that in chapter 12, the red dragon has been cast out of heaven, never to return or gain access. Therefore, it goes without saying that the devil is upset and angry that this has happened to him. He knows that his time of wickedness is just about to be over. Therefore, to bring about an evil vengeance against God, as well as on the people on earth, he brings about and empowers two Antichrist figures to wreak havoc during the second half of the tribulation period. I will first examine the Antichrist figure. Sounds familiar, Satan likes to imitate whatever God does.

John said that he saw a beast rising up out of the sea, and the beast then stood on the sands of the sea. The beast had seven heads and ten horns, and upon his horns were ten crowns, and upon the seven heads were the name of blasphemy. First of all, let me say that the King James Version said, "I stood upon the sands of the sea," depicting that it was John, since he was the one witnessing the things that must shortly come to pass. However, better manuscripts of this text use the word *he* as it was the dragon (Satan).

Some have said that this verse should have been at the end of chapter 12, because it is the devil who gives power to the beast of the sea, as well as the beast of the earth. The Greek word for *beast* is, θηριον/*therion*, meaning *animal* or *wild beast*. The word *wild* is to show the ferociousness of the beast and to show that he would not stop at anything until the appetite of his wickedness is satisfied by his devouring jaws of evil.

The beasts that are mentioned in this chapter will be ferocious, wicked, and evil and again they will be under the control and influence of the red dragon (Satan). The seventh head of the beast received a death blow, the people on his side thought he was dead, but miraculously he survived and the people were amazed. They were so astonished that it caused them to believe and to put trust in the antichrist. They even cried out and said, "Who is like unto the beast? Who is able to make war with him?"

Listen, believers of Christ: there is going to be a time when devil worship and self-glorification will be the norm. A lot of people will be deceived when they see the beast restored back to life. Just like the true and living Christ was resurrected back to life by God the Father to prove that Christ has all power and that he is Lord of Lords and Kings of Kings. It will be the devil's intention to do the same thing with the beast.

Yes, so in these verses, we see how the dragon (Satan) is behind the malicious and sinful acts of the Antichrist. The devil gave him power to make war with the saints and to destroy them. The Antichrist will have power to inflict pain and suffering over all the people of earth, and he will also try to influence the saints to follow him instead of God. There will be a great number of people who will succumb to the manipulation of the devil; those people who chose to worship him, their names will not be mentioned in the Lamb's book of life.

John then appealed to the saints to hear with understanding and discern the motive behind the Antichrist's plight, so they won't be deceived. The reign of the believers' walk will be tried and tested. Verse 10 lets us know that prison and death await those who obey God; they must hold on to their godly patience. The apostle Paul said, "Therefore, being justified by faith, we have peace with God through our Lord Jesus Christ: By whom also we have access by faith into this grace wherein we stand, and rejoice in hope of the glory of God. And not only so, but we glory in tribulation also, knowing that tribulation worketh patience and patience experience and experience hope: And hope maketh not ashamed because the love of God is shed abroad in our hearts by which is given unto us" (Ro. 5:1–5).

Looking at verse 3 again as an addendum, I would like to pose a question. Some believe that the red dragon (Satan) will resurrect the beast (Antichrist) from the dead and heal the wound that caused his fatality. But will this be a real resurrection from the dead, or will it be a fake happening or fake resurrection to validate that Satan has as much power as God? Satan, even during the tribulation period, will still try to prove his point; he will still try to exalt his throne above the heaven and be like the most high (Isa. 14:14).

Satan has a proud ego problem, but he will never be like God. He will try to pretend to be God, but he is a deceiver, a liar; he is a great illusionist. So to go along with that train of thought, it could be that the red dragon (Satan) will make people think with great wonder and subtlety that he actually brought the Antichrist back to life like God the Father did the Son (Ro. 10:5) and like Christ when he raises Lazarus from the dead (John 11:43–44).

Remember the words of the apostle Paul who said, "Even him, whose coming is after the working of Satan with all power and signs and lying wonders and with all deceivableness of unrighteousness in them that perish; because they received not the love of the truth, that they might be saved. And for this cause, God shall send them strong delusion that they should believe a lie (2 Thess. 2:9–11). The act of bringing the beast from the dead so people could follow him and look to him as god could just be a lying wonder. Note: only God the Father and Christ have the power to bring people back to life (see John 5:21, 25, 28–29).

13:11-18

In verse 11, John saw another beast coming out of the earth, and this beast had two horns like a lamb, and he spoke like a dragon. The beast in this verse is the imitator of Christ. The Antichrist is described as a lamb to falsely convey that he is the Savior of the world. Once again, he tries to compare himself to the true Messiah.

The word *lamb* is used in scripture to describe the humble ministry and sacrificial life of Jesus. The prophet Isaiah describes the suffering servant or Christ as a lamb going before a slaughter (Isa. 53:7). John said that Christ is "the Lamb of God, which taketh away the sin of the world" (John 1:29). Peter says of Christ that we "were redeemed with the precious blood of Jesus Christ like that of a lamb without blemish and without spot" (1 Pet. 1:19).

Therefore, the Antichrist is going to falsely convey to the world that he is the true lamb of his father, the true Christ, the anointed one who will come with a message of hope and love but instead will come with a ministry of evil and destruction. Jesus said, "For there shall arise false Christ, and false prophets, and shall shew great signs and wonders; insomuch that, if it were possible, they shall deceive the very elect" (Matthew 24:24).

Verse 12 lets us know that the second beast will have the same power of the first beast, or that all his power came from the first beast, which is the person that has the ability to restore the old Roman Empire. The second beast is going to be so manipulative and cunning, that he will influence the people of the earth to worship the first beast, whose deadly wounds were healed by the dragon (Satan).

The second beast is going to be so wicked and evil that he will cause fire to come down from heaven like Elijah the prophet did on Mount Carmel. When the people see these miracles, they are going to be convinced that the second beast is the true Messiah.

These signs and false miracles will lead them astray, and they will begin to worship the first beast by constructing a statue of him to be worshipped. This is to say that this beast will desire attention and praise. He will be so wicked and narcissistic that it will be all about him. In his mind, he deserves all glory and honor. When the second beast empowers the image of the first beast to come alive and speak, many will willingly worship him, and those who don't will be put to death.

The description of the first beast, as having been fatally wounded by the sword, and then having being restored back to life, is to show the dark, wicked, and illusional power of the second beast. When the unbelievers gravitate toward the evil powers of the second beast and surrender to him like a force of a strong magnet, then all who worshipped him will receive his mark upon them, either on their foreheads or upon their right hands (cf. v. 12).

These people were people of all classes of life, rich and poor. With the satanic mark of 666, they will be able to buy and sell. No trade of business would be done without it. As far as the beast's number and its interpretation, no one knows for sure. However, it's a number that is a symbolic personification of the worst type of evil manipulation and control.

14:1-5

As we begin chapter 14, let me first explain that this chapter starts with another interlude. In other words, the vision that John now sees is a proleptic one, meaning that this vision is assumed to take place sometime in the future, as opposed to the present. In other words, John saw a preview of what was going to take place within the near future. He saw the second coming of Christ, coming to earth to redeem his people and to set up his millennium kingdom. However, during this preview, details are not mentioned about him standing in Jerusalem is.

At the closing of chapter 13, the beast of the earth caused great wonders in the earth, to the point that the people of earth believed that the Antichrist is the god that they should serve and worship. As a reward and benefit, those who worship the beast would receive a mark either on their right hand or forehead, which would grant them the right to buy and sell. The mark will be the number 666. Therefore, chapter 13 paints a picture of the Antichrist as he unveils his plan of triumph.

It appears that the devil's evil scheme will be successful, but just when it appears that the devil is winning, the redeeming Christ shows up to conquer all evil. These verses demonstrate to believers that true worshippers of God can face all types of trials and tribulations with Christ at their side.

Notice the perseverance and the protection of the 144,000 in verse 1. John looked, and he saw the Lamb standing on Mount Zion, and with him were the 144,000 that had been sealed by him in their foreheads. The seal was God's name. This is to say that the 144,000 Jewish witnesses will persevere through the tribulation period, despite the Antichrist's evil plans and attacks. No wicked plan or thing will prevent them from entering the millennium kingdom.

Christ as the Lamb of God will be with them during his one-thousand-year reign on earth. This is what is meant when verse 1 tells us that a lamb stood on Mount Zion. Mount Zion is to be interpreted as Jerusalem, and since Jerusalem or the city of David is on earth, Christ will be with the 144,000 Jews, as well as with the Church to establish his millennium kingdom. Psalm 2:6 says, "Yet have I set my king upon my holy hill of Zion."

To show that the plans of the Antichrist will be destroyed and to show that the people of God will go through the seven-year tribulation period, unstopped by the devices of Satan, sounds of jubilation will take place in heaven. John heard a voice from heaven as the voice of many waters, and as the voice of a great thunder. However, John did not identify the voice. Some believe that it was the voice of the Almighty (El Shaddai) who spoke (Ezek. 1:24). We do not know for sure because, once again, John did not identify the voice. The voice could have been even an angel/beast (Rev. 7:11).

14:6–13

As we move on toward verses 6 and 7, John witnessed another angel flying in heaven. However, this angel carried a message of hope to the people on earth. The message was the everlasting gospel. God has always used angels to carry messages to His people. He used Gabriel to carry the plan of Christ's birth to Mary (Luke 1:30). Gabriel was also used to tell Zachariah about the birth of his son John (Luke 1:13–19). An angel was also used to tell Joseph about Mary's pregnancy (Matt. 1:20–24). By the way, the word *angel* in Greek is the word αγγελος/*aggelos*, meaning messenger. Therefore, God chose a heavenly messenger to bring a heavenly and truthful message.

When I read these verses, I couldn't help but think about the love that God has for people. Why? Because once again he has given man another opportunity to repent and to worship the true Messiah. Before the tribulation, Christ used prophets and the Church to point people in the direction of his saving love.

After the Rapture, he uses the 144,000 and the two witnesses to continue to spread the message of truth. Now he chooses angels to get his message of hope and love out to reach the darkness of man's wicked souls. These verses validate the truth of God's love for man. It expresses the validity of John 3:16, which says, "For God so loved the world, that he gave his only begotten son, that whosoever believeth in him should not perish, but have everlasting life." According to *Strong's Greek and Hebrew Dictionary of the Bible*, the Greek word *everlasting* is the same word in verse 6, which was used to describe the everlasting gospel, which the angel came to preach to the people of earth. It is the word αιωνιος/*aionios*, which means *eternal, forever*, "without beginning or ending," "that which will never cease," and "that which always have been and always will be."

This proves that God and his love have always been true and eternal. God and his undying love will always exist; He and his love will never cease from existence. The writer of the book of Hebrews says, "Jesus Christ is the same yesterday and today and forever" (Heb 13:8). The words that the angel used was "Fear God and give Glory to him: For the hour of his judgment is come: and worship him that made heaven, and earth, and the sea, and the fountain of waters."

After John witnessed the heavenly proclamation of the angel that carried the message of the everlasting gospel, he saw and heard another angel proclaim, "Babylon is fallen, is fallen, that great city, because she made all nations drink of the wine of the wrath of her fornication." In order to understand this verse, we must first understand the identity of Babylon. Some have suggested that the city Babylon is to be taken literally; some have interpreted the Roman Empire to be Babylon. Some have suggested that it is perhaps Jerusalem.

It is my belief that Babylon is to be interpreted as the Roman Empire. I say this because the apostle Peter said, "The church that is at Babylon, elected together with you, saluteth you; and so doth Marcus my son" (1 Peter 5:13). When Peter said this, the Babylonian empire was no longer in existence. Peter used Babylon as a symbolic reference of the evil of Rome. In other words, it was Rome that existed in Peter's time and not Babylon.

John the revelator sees another angel, and that angel had a message of doom. He said, "If any man worships the beast and his image and receive his mark in his forehead, or in his hand, the same shall drink of the wine of the wrath of God, which is poured out without mixture into the cup of his indignation: and he shall be tormented with fire and brimstone in the presence of the holy angels, and in the presence of the Lamb."

I feel that this is to be interpreted as God telling the people of earth that if they chose to worship the beast as opposed to worshipping Christ as the Messiah, that eternal damnation awaits them in hell. This message of doom is a warning to all those who will not take heed to the message of the everlasting gospel.

If they do not take heed to refuse to worship the Antichrist, then they will feel the wrath of God's judgment. Revelation 21:8 says, "But the fearful, and unbelieving, and the abominable, and murderers, and sorcerers, and idolaters, and all liars, shall have their part in the lake which burneth with fire and brimstone: which is the second death." Verse 11 reminds us that those who are eternally sentenced into hell will be eternally punished in hell forever.

This is evident because the shrieking cries of their sufferings will arise from the lake of fire like smoke from an erupting volcano. The words "they have no rest day or night" prove the continued plight of their oncoming and eternal doom. Listen, beloved of Christ, when Christians have their days of trials, they know that joy is to come in the morning (Ps. 30:5), but there will be no future joy for those who are hell bound; weep and gnashing of the teeth will be their painful and daily acquaintance. Jesus said, "But the children of the kingdom shall be cast out into darkness: there shall be weeping and gnashing of teeth" (Matt. 8:12).

Verses 12 and 13 validates the security of the souls of those who are genuinely in Christ. Those who endure with their faith in Christ during the tribulation period and obey his word will have an eternal resting place with him in heaven.

14:14–20

As John continued to look, he saw a white cloud, and sitting upon the cloud he saw one that appeared to him to be the son of man. This man had upon his head a golden crown, and he held in his hand a sharp sickle. It goes without saying that the person riding or sitting upon this white cloud is that of Christ. The crown that he wears is symbolic of his royal position as a righteous judge and by him having a sickle in his hands validate that. What is a sickle? Well, a sickle is a short, curved metal blade with a short handle, and it is use for agricultural purposes.

It is used metaphorically in most scriptures to depict God's judgment. Notice what Jeremiah said in the prophecy of his book. He said, "Cut off the sower from Babylon, and him that handleth the sickle in the time of harvest" (Jer 50:16). Notice what John said when it came to using a sickle metaphorically to talk about God's wrath and judgment. He said, "And I looked, and behold a white cloud, and upon the cloud sat like unto the Son of man, having on his head a golden crown, and in his hand a sharp sickle" (Rev. 14:14).

The war of Armageddon will be a war that will not be isolated in one area, but it will be a battle that will spread throughout the land of Palestine.

15:1-8

As we move forward to discuss the fifteenth chapter of this prophetic book, let me begin by saying that this is the shortest chapter of Revelation. However, within its eight sentences lies the wrath of God's judgments. During this portion of the tribulation period, these severe penalties will be carried out by seven angels with plagues ready to be unleashed upon the rebellious unsaved. But before that, John noticed a sign in heaven. The word *sign* in the Greek is the word σημεῖον /*semeion,* and it means a miracle for a specific purpose or end, an unusual purpose or happening, a sign that indicates something, or a manifestation of the supernatural power of God for a reason.

John also used the word *marvelous*, which is the word θαυμαστός /*thaumastós* in the Greek language. This word indicates that there was a wonderful thing done in heaven or something marvelous that took place; a great wonder. Within the vision that John saw was a sea of glass mingled with fire and them that had gotten the victory. This is to say that the tribulation saints did not waver in their faith in Christ once they recognized that Jesus is the true messiah. The sea of glass is symbolic of their transparent faith in Christ. Listen, my friends, we should walk and live so close to Christ that people can see our faith in Christ. Jesus said in Matthew 5:16, "Let your light so shine before men that they may see your good works, and glorify your Father which is in heaven."

The word *fire* depicts the intense persecution that they will endure from the attacks of the Antichrist. Like Polycarp who refused not to deny Christ, even as he was bound to stake of flame, and when they saw that the fire did not consume his body, they stabbed him. Yes, my Christian friends, the tribulation saints had gotten the victory over the beast. As they stood on the sea of glass (their faith), they sang the song of Moses (Ex. 15) and the song of the Lamb (1 Cor. 5:7; 1 Pet. 1:19). They worshipped and praise God by singing, "Great and marvelous are thy works, Lord God almighty; just and true are thy ways, thou king of saints."

Their songs of praise represent their redemption and deliverance. When this song was sung in Exodus 15 and Deuteronomy 32, it was to show how God released them from a physical bondage from Egypt. However, in this passage of scripture, it was sung to celebrate God releasing them from a spiritual bondage; it was sung to praise God from protecting them from the spiritual wickedness of the devil

John, the beloved disciple, looked again, and he saw within the temple of God that the Tabernacle of the Testimony was open in heaven. What was this testimony that was open in the temple of heaven? It is the law of God that that was used by Moses from God to show Israel, as well as nonbelievers, how far they were from God. Israel had a temple on earth patterned after the temple in heaven (Exod. 25:40). And within their temple—behind the veil, behind the holy place, which led to the holiest of holy places—was kept the Ark of the Covenant, and within the Ark of the Covenant was the table of stone, which was written God's law.

It was from the law of God that the people of earth were to be judged. To carry out this judgment, Christ allowed seven angels to carry seven last plagues to bring judgment to the people of earth. For further clarification, the Greek word for *plague* is the word πληγη/ *plege*, meaning "to cause a public calamity," "to wound," "to cause strife," and "to cause heavy affliction." These angels were about to cause severe affliction of the worst kind to the people of the earth. They were dressed in pure white linen, perhaps studded with precious stones. The garment upon their breast was fastened together with a golden belt or girdle. By the description of their attire, one would think that it's the attire of a priest who brings about mercy, comfort, and hope, but these angels and their mission was not to bring mercy, but that of judgment.

One of the four beasts that was in God's temple came forward and presented, to the seven angels, seven golden vials or bowls, which was full of the wrath of God to the seven angels. This is not the first time that golden bowls was used in scripture. Gold bowls were used to hold the prayers of the saints in chapter 5:8; the Old Testament priest of Israel used gold bowls in their temple service (1 Kings 7:50; 2 Kings 12:13, 25:15). After the angels received the bowls of judgment from the beast, the temple of God was filled with smoke to depict God's presence and power (Exod. 19:18, 40:34; 1 Kings 8:10–11; 2 Chron. 5:11–14, 7:1–3; Isa. 6:4; Ezek. 11:23, 44:4). His presence so engulfed his temple that no one was allowed to go inside the temple until the last seven plagues were fulfilled.

I feel that the reason why no one was allowed to go inside the temple was to reinforce the fact that the glorious Lord was behind this work of judgment and that no mercy was to be given; God's mind was made up—the tribulation period was soon to be completed by the seven vials of his wrath.

During that time, the mercy of God will not be visible; only destruction of the worst kind will be manifested, and nothing will detour God away from his judgment. Remember, the number seven means completeness, and God will complete his judgment of woes toward the evil and wicked of the earth.

16:1–16

Chapter 16 opens up with the seven angels, with their seven bowls of judgment, which are the wrath of God upon unbelievers on earth. Christ, in his commanding voice, sends out these seven angels of the apocalypse like a general who sends out orders of attack to his soldiers against those of the opposing side. As the first angel responded to Christ, the commander in chief, he went out and poured out his bowl of wrath upon the earth.

The results were that of noisome and grievous sore upon the unbelievers, which had the mark of the beast, and were actively involved in worshipping his image. The Greek word for *noisome* is the word κοκας/*kakos*, meaning "that which is troublesome," "to cause injuries," *destructive*, and *harm*; it also means *evil* and *wicked*.

As John witnessed the second angel obeying the command of that great voice, the angel poured out his vial upon the sea, and the sea became as blood to depict death. Everything that was in the sea died. This bowl of judgment resembled the first plague that was cast upon Egypt when Pharaoh refused to let God's people go (Exod. 7:20–25). In Revelation 8:8, as the second angel sounded his trumpet, a mountain burning with fire was cast into the sea, and the third part of the sea became blood. But in Revelation 16:3, all of earths seas will be affected. In other words, this bowl of judgment will be far worse and severe than that of Revelation 8:8.

John also saw the third angel pouring out his bowl of judgment and from that the rivers and upon all the fresh water supply, and it became blood as well. Listen, mankind cannot live without water, just like mankind cannot live a complete, joyous, and spirit-fill life unless he drinks from the fountain of Christ, who is the living water. After the angel poured out his bowl of judgment upon the earth, John heard him say, "Thou art righteous, o Lord, which art, and wast, and shall be, because thou hast judged thus. For they have shed the blood of saints and prophets, and thou hast given them blood to drink; for they are worthy."

This is to say that the third angel was in total agreement with the judgments of God. He praises Christ for being eternal; he praises him for his righteousness, as well as his righteous acts of judgments, simply because those who were on the side of the Antichrist shed the innocent blood of Christs' righteous ones, and it is because of this reason that their blood will be shed as well. John heard other voices agreeing with the righteous judgments of Christ, sounding from the altar of God. I believe that these voices were the tribulation saints who were crying out to God underneath his altar. At last, vengeance had finally come to them (see Rev. 6:9–11).

John then saw a fourth angel pouring out his vial upon the sun, and when he did that, he was given power to scorch the unbelievers of earth. The Greek word for *scorch* is the word καυματιζω/*kaumatizo*, meaning "to burn with heat," "to scorch," and "to be tortured with intense heat." Believers of Christ, it goes without saying that no amount of sunblock would protect the unbelievers from the sunburn of God's wrath. But nevertheless, despite their burning torment, they still will not repent from their evil and turn to God; they will go so far as to blaspheme Christ for what he has done to them (see Deut 32:24; Isa. 24:6; Isa. 42:25; Mal 4:1).

The fifth angel poured out his bowl of judgment upon the seat of the beast because the Antichrist's kingdom was full of evil, wickedness, and darkness. Their pain was so severe that they gnawed their tongue. The Greek word for *gnawed* is the word μασαομαι/*massaomai*, meaning "to chew," "to consume," "to eat," and "to devour." The unbelievers of earth are going to be in so much pain that they are going to bite and chew their tongue severely. In other words, the gnawing of their tongue is going to be a reaction of reflex of their agonizing pain.

The six angels poured out his bowl of judgment upon the River Euphrates, and the water completely dried up.

Before we go on to the seventh seal, let me first say that once again there is a break, an interlude between the sixth and the seventh bowl of judgment. What John saw during the intermission were three unclean spirits like frogs that came out of the mouth of the dragon, and out of the mouth of the beast, and out of the mouth of the false prophet.

These spirits like frogs were demons that were working miracles, which go forth upon the kings of the earth to give them ability together with the nations on the earth to battle against God almighty. We know that the dragon is the devil, the beast is the Antichrist, but who is the false prophet? Revelation 13:13–14 speaks of the second beast, the beast from the land that performs wonders and miracles to convince the people of earth to worship the first beast, which is the Antichrist. Therefore, the works of the second beast is no other than the false prophet that is mentioned in 16:13. It is my opinion that the devil, the Antichrist, and the false prophet will deceive the nations with lying words and join them together with false signs and wonders to get them to war against God. The demons will be like that of frogs.

Frogs were a plague against Egypt (see Exodus 8:5–1; Psalm 105:30). They were unclean, according to the list in Leviticus 11:10.

In verse 15, John hears Christ say that he was coming as a thief, and those who are blessed are those who watch and keep his garments.

Verse 16 tells us that God gathered them to a place called, in the Hebrew tongue, Armageddon. The place, Armageddon or Megiddo, was the location where many ancient battles were fought.

17-21

John heard a voice that came from the temple of God in heaven. I feel that this voice is no other than Christ's. I say that because he used the words "it is done" as if he completed a task of a great assignment. The Greek definition for the words "it's done" is the same definition for the words "it's finished," words in which Christ said when he completed his work of atonement when he was crucified on the cross. However, when he said the words "it is done," it is to show that the judgments that he pronounced during the tribulation period had now ended for the people, as well as for the Antichrist on earth.

When the angel poured out his bowl upon the earth, there was lightning, thundering, and a great earthquake. This earthquake will be so enormous, that it would devastate the entire world. In other words, this earthquake is going to be so mighty, that the structure of the earth will be completely changed. Jerusalem will be divided into three parts. The extent of the earth will affect Babylon, which will be destroyed because of their wickedness. There will be hails as well, weighing from 56 to 114 pounds. Instead of men repenting, they will blaspheme God.

17:1-2

Chapter 17 starts out by John saying that one of the seven angels, which carried the seven vials, came out and talked to him and said that he will show him the judgments that will befall the great whore what sits upon the many waters. The great whore is that of the unsaved, who go through the tribulation period. It is also known as the false Church or the superficial Church that appears to be saved on the outside but whose members have not repented of their sins, they have not accepted Christ on the inside of their hearts; they have a form of godliness, but they deny the true doctrine of Jesus Christ by not living a godly lifestyle.

The great harlot or the false church will affect many nations, like leaven that affects and spreads through bread. When it comes to false teaching, Jesus said, "Take heed and beware of the leaven of the Pharisees and of the Sadducees" (Matt. 16:6).

17:3-7

Once again, we see John being carried away into the wilderness. As he was in the spirit, he saw within his vision a woman sitting on a scarlet beast, full of names of blasphemy, having seven heads and ten horns. The woman again is symbolic of Babylon as a false religious system or the restored Roman Empire. The wilderness could be interpreted as the desolate condition of the false religious system (the woman), or it can be a literal wilderness because around Babylon and Rome lies a wilderness (see Isaiah 47–48 and Jeremiah 50–51). The beast is the Antichrist, who heads the restored Roman Empire. Rome at this time will be the center of all the religions of the world; it will be noted as the one world order with one religion that will be a mixture of all the religions of the world. Rome will be known, in other words, as the religious capital of the world. The true Church was Raptured, and on earth is the false church that will accept all religions and blend them into one. This belief goes against the doctrine of Christianity. Jesus said, "I am the way, the truth and the life, no man can get to the Father, except come go by me" (John 14:6).

17:8-10

Many people believe that the beast "that was" speaks about the Roman Empire's history. The Roman Empire was an empire that was to be feared in the world. No one conquered it; it fell apart from the inside. I also believe that the words "shall ascend out of the bottomless pit" means that the Roman Empire will be restored by the wicked power of the Antichrist. However, when that happens, it won't be long until the coming Christ will destroy his plan of restoration and wickedness.

17:11-14

The angel also said, "The beast that was, and is not, even he is the eight, and is of the seven, and goeth into perdition." This is making reference to not only the restored Roman Empire, but also to the Antichrist, who will be the satanic force behind it. He is the little horn in Daniel 7:7-8, 23-26. The Antichrist will be so in charge that he is considered to be the eighth feature of the empire.

17:15-18

Within these verses, the whore or the restored Roman Empire who sits upon the waters will be in control and will rule all nations; for the waters represent all ethnic groups of people. However, it will only be temporary, for the ten horns who are the ten kings that rule over parts of the Roman Empire will be controlled by the Antichrist. They will turn their allegiance over to the Antichrist.

Again, this allegiance will be short-lived; the pride of the Antichrist will be so narcissistic that it will cause him to share his glory with no one. He will destroy the whore, which is the false religious system and who is also known as the Roman Empire. He alone will be worshipped and no one else. He will also break his peace treaty with Israel and destroy the whore.

18:1-3

Chapter 18 opens its prophetic curtain with a message against proud Babylon. It's a message of devastation that will warn Babylon of its oncoming doom. However, this is not the only scripture that eludes to the demise of that city. There are prophetic scriptures all through the Old Testament that talks of its doom. Scriptures such as Isaiah 13:19-22; Jeremiah 50:39, 51:37 to name just a few.

This prophetic woe was announced by a great angel of God coming down from heaven, and as he ascended down to the earth, a splendor of light of his glory shone upon the earth. The light that is mentioned could be symbolic of the presence and authority of God. No matter how a person tries to cover up their darkness, the light of the Lord will reveal their wickedness, then judgment will surely come. Jesus said, "This is the judgment, that the light has come into the world, and men loved the darkness rather than the light, for their deeds were evil (John 3:19).

Babylon, which could be prophetically Rome, was lifted up in pride; their evil deeds influenced other nations to follow them in their wrongdoings. Demonic activity, as well as wickedness, was their daily norm; but woe unto the nation that thinks that wrong is right and right is wrong. God's judgment will come. As the great and mighty angel descended upon the earth, he declared with a strong and authoritative voice: "Babylon the great has fallen, is fallen, and has become the habitation of devils...

18:4-6

As I attempt to elaborate upon these verses, I noticed the compassionate voice of another angel, which reflects the merciful and compassionate character of Christ. The angelic call of mercy was given to God's people, who allowed the seducing lifestyle of Babylon to entice them into wickedness. The words "Come ye out" was a command, as well as an invitation, of love for the people of God to repent of their sins and come back to God.

Isn't it a blessing to know that the call of God's love is open to all those who love God and to those who are open to his call? It doesn't matter how dark their sins may be, or how far they are away from God; all they have to sincerely do is to confess their sins and repent and turn back to God. The apostle John said, "If we confess our sin, he is faithful and just to forgive us our sins and to cleanse us from all unrighteousness" (1 John 1:9).

When Moses came down from Mount Sinai, he noticed God's people being influenced by evil doings and participating in wickedness. Instead of asking God to destroy the whole tribe, Moses gave a call of repentance by saying, "Who is on the Lord's side? Let him come unto me..." (Exod. 32:26). However, whenever God's call of love was not accepted, consequences followed. The voice explained to the people of earth that if they did not adhere to the call of God, then they will be judged with the same judgment of wicked Babylon. As believers of Christ, we must strive to live holy and righteous lives before Christ. The apostle Paul said, "Be ye not unequally yoke with unbelievers: for what fellowship hath righteousness with unrighteouness? And what communion hath light with darkness?" He advised his son Timothy to "neither be partaker of another men's sins: Keep thyself pure" (1 Tim 5:22b).

18:7–10

As we go through these verses, I want you to notice the pride and arrogance of Babylon. Notice her mindset: "I sit a queen, and am no widow, and shall see no sorrow." Babylon was full of self-deception. She thought that she was untouchable; she thought that because she was living and enjoying the fruit of her wicked labor, that she would never have to depend on others for help or for sustainability like widows are accustomed to. Like a queen who lived a life of luxury, she thought that she would never be uncomfortable and that sorrow would never be beyond her horizon.

But oh, was she ever so wrong! Needless to say, sorrow, destruction, torment, and misery was about to receive her like a mother who opens her arms to receive her newborn child for the very first time. But instead of receiving a bundle of joy, sorrow and grief will be her bundle of pain. Listen, saints of God, when living a life of sin and evil, no one is exempt from the chastening hand of God. There is a heavy price to pay. Plagues, famine, and the fiery judgment of God will be their demise. The Psalmist said in Psalm 145:20: "The Lord keeps all who love him, But, all the wicked He will destroy." Nations and their leaders, who once followed her into immorality and who stood in awe of her glory, were now in awe of her destruction. Before I imagine, they were once praising her because of her glory, but now they were lamenting her because of her calamity. They were once close to her because of her seducing spirit and lifestyle, but now they were standing far off and saying, "Alas, alas that great city of Babylon, that mighty city! For in one hour is thy judgment come."

18:11–19

These verses give us a picture of all the people and businesses who depended upon Babylon for their financial livelihood. Because Babylon was destroyed in a matter of sixty minutes, merchants who bought from her saw their life over as well. They too were doomed to a life of misery, pain, and poverty. They voiced their deep disappointment by saying, "Alas. Alas, that great city that was clothed in fine linen, and purple, and scarlet, and decked with gold, and precious stones, and pearls! For in one hour, so great riches is come to nought…"

18:20–24

The same angelic voice of heaven that pronounced judgment upon Babylon, and encouraged the people of God to repent from their evil ways of Babylon, is the same heavenly voice that we see in these verses that encourage the people of God to rejoice over Babylon's demise. As believers and followers of Christ, we should rejoice and give praise to God when he defeats our enemies. We should praise God for giving us all the victories in our lives. Did not the Lord say, "Vengence is mine, saith the Lord, I will repay" (Psalm 37:1–2; Isa. 63:4; Rom 12:19).

To show God's vengeance upon Babylon, another powerful angel came upon the scene and picked up a great boulder that resembled a millstone and cast it into the sea. The word *millstone* is used to show the devastation of God's judgment upon Babylon. In the Greek language, the word *millstone* is μυλος/*mulos*, meaning "to grind or crush." This is to say that the judgment of God is going to crush Babylon, along with its false worship and evil works to the point where they will exist no more. It is to also say that the people who idolized them will hear the sounds of their judgment.

They will say, "with violence shall that great city Babylon be thrown down, and shall be found no more at all." At one time, the city of Babylon was a city of excitement and glory, but now it will be known as a city of desolation. No longer will there be parties of joy, no longer will there be sounds of elation in the streets, and no longer will there be sounds of music in the streets; this all would be replaced with sounds of agony and pain. Rejoice! Because the blood of all the prophets and the saints that were spilled by Babylon will be avenged. Jesus said, "Blessed are ye, when men shall revile you, and persecute you, and shall say all manner of evil against you falsely, for my sake. Rejoice and be exceeding glad: for great is your reward in heaven: for so persecuted they the prophets which were before you" (Matt. 5:11–12).

19:1-5

Moving on to chapter 19, John begin by saying, "And after these things." What things? The Greek words are *meta tauta*, meaning the things that have already happened or transpired. What had transpired in the previous chapter was the destruction of mystical Babylon, that great apostate system that influenced the nations to drink the wine of her fornication; it was destroyed by the lamb in one hour (17:14; 18:16–20).

The words "after these things" also give us a hint that something else is getting ready to take place. What things? Things like a victory celebration in heaven, as well as the marriage supper of the Lamb. Celebrations of praise because the tribulation period had ended, and to show the jubilant appreciation for what Christ had done, many people in heaven will join in to praise God for what he has done. To show the vast number, as well as the multitude, who begin to praise God, there are two Greek words that are to be considered.

First the word *great* in Greek is the word μεγας/*megas*, meaning "large in number and quantity." It is also to show great effort; it is to show the affection and emotions of the mind. Second, the word *much* in Greek is the word πολλος /*polos*, meaning *many, much*, or "large in number" or *multitude*. The people who were a part of this great and large praise team of heaven was made up of heaven's best, like the twenty-four elders, the four beasts, as well as the tribulation saints. All joined in and gave God the very best of praise. They sang, "Alleluia: salvation, and glory, and honor, and power unto the Lord our God." Let's examine these words to find out the true meaning of what they were saying.

The word *Alleluia* in the Greek language is the word $αλληλουια$/*alleluia*, meaning "to praise God." It's an invitation to praise *yah*. *Yah* is the shortened form of Yahweh. It is also the most holy name for God in the Old Testament. Alleluia is also the transliteration of the Hebrew word *Hallelujah*. It's an invitation to praise Jehovah or God. Hallelujah is the highest praise that one can render to God. In other words, all the heavenly hosts were invited to join in to praise the most Holy God for what he has done and for what he was about to do.

When the heavenly team used the word *salvation*, it was used to give recognition to Christ as Savior and deliverer. For truly he saved and delivered his saints from the wicked grips of Babylon and from the power of the Antichrist. When they used the word *glory*, it was to show that they have a high opinion of Christ. The Greek word is $δοξα$/*doxa*, meaning having a high opinion, resulting in praise and honor.

When the saints of God thought about all what Christ had done, it brought nothing but good thoughts of him to the point that they gave him all the glory. When they used the word *honor* to go with their lyrics of praise, it was to show that God should be held in reverence at all times. In Greek, it is the word $τιμη$/*time*/*tee-may*, meaning *honor*, which belongs or is shown to one. It means to respect or to hold in reverence. When they used the word *power*, they conveyed that the enemy was destroyed by the supernatural and divine ability of God.

The Greek word for *power* is the word $δυναμις$/*dunamis*, meaning *strength*, *power*, and *ability*. When they used the word *Lord* in their song, they were validating Christ as their owner, their Lord, and their master. The Greek word is $κυριος$/*kurios*, meaning *master*, *owner*, *Lord*. Saints of God, if there is anything that ensembles and choirs should validate in their worship songs, it's showing praise, loyalty, and ownership to God, as they worship him in spirit and in truth.

David said, "Make a joyful noise unto the Lord, all ye lands. Serve the Lord with gladness: come before his presence with singing. Know ye that the Lord he is God: it is he that hath made us, and not we ourselves; we are his people, and the sheep of his pasture. Enter into his gates with thanksgiving, and into his courts with praise: be thankful unto him, and bless his name. For the Lord is good; his mercy everlasting; and his truth endureth to all generations" (Psalm 100:1–5).

Again, the reason for this high praise is directed toward God is because Christ has defeated and destroyed that great whore, Babylon. God annihilated Babylon with the truth and righteousness of his judgments. Yes. God is righteous and true. This speaks of his divine attribute. He is righteous because the Psalmist said, "The Lord is righteous in all his ways, and holy in all his works" (Psalm 145:17).

God is true because John the beloved disciple said, "And we know that the Son of God is come, and hath given us an understanding, that we may know him that is true, and we are in him that is true, even in his Son Jesus Christ. This is the true God, and eternal life" (1 John 5:20). The only way that God works and operates is through the true nature of his character. It's against God's nature to be unfair, untruthful, and unjust.

God judges the hearts of people by and through his own holy standards. He will do this to avenge the blood of his faithful saints. Wouldn't that be a blessing if all believers could learn the valuable lesson of praising the highest God? Praise changes the atmosphere of worship. It places all the attention on God. It reminds us of who God is; it reminds us of the beauty of his holiness.

In this case, the heavenly host is praising God because Babylon will never rise again. The smoke of her demise is a reminder that they are a defeated foe, never to return again. As they continued to praise God, the twenty-four elders and the four beasts fell down and worshipped God, saying amen, Alleluia. They were in agreement with the praise celebration that was going on. Made no difference on how long the praise went on, they knew that God was worthy of the praise.

After the twenty-four elders and the four living creatures fell down to praise and worship the only true God, a voice came out from the throne of God, saying, "Praise our God, all ye his servants, and ye that fear him, both small and great."

If there is anything that dedicated Christian love to do every day, it's to praise God sincerely and wholeheartedly, especially after God has given them victories in their life. Praise songs such as these are called paean songs of praise to show deep appreciation to God for giving them victory, peace, and elation. This is another reason why we, as believers, should sing a paean praise to God. Again, a paean praise is the most profound praise directed toward God. According to *Webster's Dictionary*, the word *paean* is a song of joy, peace, or victory. It is also: (1) A joyous song or hymn of praise, tribute, thanksgiving, or triumph (2) a work that praises or honors its subject.

It goes without saying that the subject in this case is Christ. He has defeated the false religious institution Babylon, and now he makes ready for his marriage to his church. Beloved, this heavenly choir lifted up their voices to depict victory, triumph, and honor to God. Listen, have you ever been to a wedding where the lyrics and the melody of the song depict sadness, dryness, and gloom? Where the crooner sang the blues rather than singing about love and happiness? I hope not. Songs at wedding ceremonies should tell the story of happiness, joy, and love! It should be indicative of the joyful relationship that is occurring and that will last forever.

I remember when I got married over thirty-four years ago to the most beautiful girl in the world (Nadine). We sung the gospel song "To God Be the Glory." As we serenaded each other at the altar, we felt the anointing of God's presence, which validated to us that our marriage was to last forever.

When John heard the heavenly voices praising God for the purpose of triumph and victory, it was a joyful sound that he could have enjoyed forever. Matter of fact, the multitude was so loud that it sounded like thunder and roared like the sound of many waters. Verse 6 tells us that they praised God for being omnipotent. What does that mean? In the Greek language, it is the word παντοκράτωρ/ *pantokrátōr*; meaning *power, strength*, and d*ominion*. "Ruler over all," *omnipotent, almighty,* "spoken only of God (2 Cor 6:18; Rev. 1:8, 4:8, 11:17, 15:3, 16:7, 14; 19:6, 15; 21:22; 2 Sam 5:10, 7:25, 27; Job 5:17, 8:5). As believers, we are not to be ashamed to lift up our voices unto the heavens. We are within God's will to make a joyful sound unto the Lord; for truly God has done and is doing great things. The heavenly choir was also praising God because of Christ's marriage to the church. John hears them sing in verses 7–8, "Let us be glad and rejoice, and give honor to him; for the marriage of the lamb is come, and his wife hath made herself ready." This is to be interpreted as a divine relationship that will be between all believers from the time that the Church was established on the day of Pentecost, all the way up unto the Rapture of the Church. To show the jubilant praise that is directed to Christ and his bride, the church, let us define the word alleluia in the Greek. It is the word ἀλληλούϊα/ ***allēlloúia,*** meaning to praise and to celebrate Yahweh or Jehovah. This word is also used in temple worship. This lets me know that one of the greatest things that believers can do within their church services is to praise and celebrate God for the things that he has done and for the things that he is going to do. Also, the word alleluia/praise was also used in the beginning of some psalm of praise (Psalm 33:2, 104:35, 35:18, 69:30, 106:1), to name just a few. It was also used to commemorate and honor God's decisive judgment upon the evil workers who refuse to accept Christ as Savior and King. The psalmist said, "Let the sinners be consumed out of the earth, and let the wicked be no more. Bless thou the Lord, O my soul. Praise ye the Lord" (Ps. 104:35).

As this wedding celebration takes place, notice how the bride (church) is dressed. They are dressed in fine linen, meaning the best of white apparel. This is to show that the church has endured by their faith in Christ. Also, it is to depict that their righteous deeds will be rewarded by Christ. The apostle Paul makes reference of the church (believers) being judged based upon their righteous works when he said, "For we must all appear before the judgement seat of Christ; that everyone may receive the things done in his body, whether it be good or bad" (2 Cor. 5:10). Notice that I said that their righteous deeds will be rewarded in Christ because without Christ we could do nothing. Jesus said, "I am the vine, ye are the branches. He that abideth in me, and I in him, the same bringeth fourth much fruit: for without me ye can do nothing" (John 15:5).

Then, too, to show the validity of God's grace upon the frailty of man's inability to perfect and create their own righteousness, the prophet Isaiah said, "But we are all as an unclean thing, and all our righteousness are as filthy rags, and we all do fade as a leaf; and our iniquities, like the wind have, have taken us away" (Isa. 64:6). Yes, my friend, the believers (church) righteous acts are only made possible through our Lord and Savior Jesus Christ. To bear witness of this truth, notice what Paul tells the church at Philippi, as well as us today. He said, "And be found in him, not having mine own righteousness, which is of the law, but that which is through the faith of Christ, the righteousness which is of God by faith" (Philippians 3:9).

Now the marriage of the lamb (Jesus) to the bride (church) is going to take place in heaven, where as the supper or the reception is going to take place on earth and all believers, as well as those believers who kept the faith during the tribulation period will be invited to celebrate this momentous occasion. This celebration will occur during the millennium period when the devil will be bound in the bottomless pit for a thousand years and when Christ will set up his kingdom. People of Christ from all races will be there to take part in this joyous festivity.

Listen, followers of Christ. How many times have you participated or heard of a festive celebration when everyone was in a celebratory mindset and then all of a sudden, an argument, a fight, or some other type of boisterous disagreement broke out to disrupt the joyous occasion? I just witnessed on the news that Joe Biden has just been voted to be the next president elect. When CNN made the announcement, people from all over the United States began to go out into the streets to celebrate his victory. However, during this same time when they were celebrating, there were some of Trump's supporters who opposed the news and they went out into the streets to protest and to show that they were not in agreement with that decision.

I say this to point out that when the marriage supper, as well as the reception, takes place for Christ and his new bride, there will be no conflicts, struggles, or protests. Why? Because the devil will not be allowed to show up. Remember, he will be bound in the bottomless pit for a thousand years. What a celebration that will be, when everyone will be on one accord without the demonic presence of the devil. After hearing that truth saying from the angelic being, John fell down to worship him. However, the angelic being told him to get up, for he is not to be worshipped. Only God, he said, is to be worshipped. David said, "O come, let us worship and bow down: let us kneel before the Lord our maker" (Psalm 95:6).

God is the only God to be adored and worshipped. If any man does otherwise, then it's idolatry. Jesus said to Satan when he was being tempted by him, "Thou shalt worship the Lord thy God and him only shalt thou serve" (Matt. 4:10).

19:11-16

As we look as these verses, we see once again that John has been given an invitation to witness and see in heaven. We know this is true by the words "And I saw heaven open." As you know, this is not the first time that heaven was opened to John. In chapter 4, a door was open in heaven, and John heard a voice sounding like a trumpet. He was invited to come up and witness the things that were going to take place. In chapter 11:19, the temple of God was open in heaven, and John saw the Ark of the Covenant. In chapter 15:5, the temple of the Tabernacle of the Testimony was open to him.

When John looked, he saw a white horse. The rider on the horse was called faithful and true. John also said that "in righteousness doth he judged and make war." What a great statement John made; this statement validates the Christians' victory. It also validates the destruction of evil and wickedness. Notice how Christ makes his entrance. He rode upon a white horse, and his name was called faithful and true. A white horse is the animal of battle; it's the animal of choice in which one rode to declare and to show victory.

Christ came to make war and to defeat the enemy. The color white in the Greek language is the word λευκος/leukos, meaning "white, glittering, and shining" (Matt. 17:3, 28:3; Mark 9:3). The

Greek word for *faithful* is the word πιστος/*pistos*, meaning "to win over," "to persuade," "worthy of belief," *trust*, or *confidence*. The Greek definition of these two words leads us to believe that when Christ takes his victory ride on that white horse, he will fulfill all believers' hope that they have in him. Him riding on that white horse will prove that he is trustworthy and faithful. The Greek word for *true* is the word αληθινος/*alethinos*, meaning "one who cannot lie," *true*, and "one who is genuine and real," as opposed to that which is false (John 4:37, 14:6, 19:35).

This word *true*, then, lets us as believers know that when Christ comes back, he will judge the world truthfully and in righteousness. He is real and genuine; he cannot lie nor can he be bribed. Christ is the paramount of truth. The words "His eyes were as a flame of fire" is to be interpreted as him judging the ungodliness of the world. In Chapter 1:14, Christ was described as having "eyes as a flame" to describe him as judging the seven Churches of Asia.

When Christ rides on that beast of war, he will seriously come for business, and that is to judge all evil. He will not come to play but to set things in order. John also saw many crowns upon Christ's head. This is to say that Christ will come to rule the world as the King of Kings and Lord of Lords, and his followers will be obliged to do what he says.

John went on further to describe Christ's vesture as being dipped in blood. His vesture is his garments, and the blood speaks of him destroying and shedding the blood of the wicked. This was not his blood that was shed on Calvary, because when he lived on earth, he was led as a lamb to the slaughter, a feat that allowed him to freely lay down his life. However, when he comes to earth the second time, he will be the lion of Judah that will shred his enemies to pieces.

He will come as the King of Kings to declare victory over those who have been rebelling against him. The prophet Isaiah said this prophetically about Christ hundreds of years before Christ's birth and crucifixion. He said, "I trod them in my anger, and trampled them in my wrath; their blood is sprinkled upon my garments, and I have stained all my raiment" (Isaiah 63:1–3).

John said his name is called the Word of God. Based on John 1:1,14, the word in this text is no other than Jesus Christ our Savior. He is the same Word of God—Jesus that will destroy and defeat the evil wicked when he comes to earth after the tribulation period.

During that time period, armies will follow him to earth. The armies will consist of the angels of heaven, the Church, the tribulation saints, as well as the Old Testament saints. Their fine linen that they wore depicts their righteousness in Christ.

Christ will judge the wicked with the pureness of his word. No one will talk his way out of his judgments. God's word is true and just. The writer of Hebrews said, "For the Word of God is quick, and powerful, and sharper than any two-edged sword, piercing even to the dividing asunder of souls and spirit, and of the joint and marrow, and is a discerner of the thoughts and intents of the heart. Neither is there any creature that is not manifest in his sight: but all things are naked and opened unto the eyes of him with whom we have to do" (Hebrews 4:12).

The word *winepress* is to show Christ's wrath and his crushing judgment that he will have against all the wicked nations that will oppose him. David said, "You shall break them with a rod of iron, and dash them in pieces like a potter's vessel" (Psalm 2:9). Written on the garments/robe of Christ, and upon his thigh, are the words "King of Kings, and Lord of Lords." The robe is symbolic of a royal majesty, and the thigh is a symbol of power. In essence, the robe that Christ wore extended over his thigh for all to see. Christ is the ultimate royal majesty, and when he comes, he will come in ultimate supernatural power to conquer and put an end to all evil and wickedness.

19:17–18

These verses tell us how Christ is going to get rid of all the carcasses of the wicked. John saw an angel standing in the sun. He heard him summon all the flesh-eating birds, like the vultures, to eat the dead bodies of the wicked (cf. Ezek. 39:4, 17–20). The feast is called the great supper of God.

The supper is not the same as the marriage supper of the Lamb, for the marriage supper of the Lamb is a time of great festive joy. The supper of the great God is a time when the wrath of God will be so harsh and severe that dead bodies will cover the face of the earth. The judgment of God will be so severe that God will call upon the carrion-eating fowls to eat them up. No body of any rebelling king, or captain, would be spared from this earth-cleansing venture. No flesh from any wicked person will be left as a memorial of this seven-year act of evil.

19:19–21

The three verses of this chapter show the coming defeat of the Antichrist, as well as the victorious power of the conquering Christ. It shows that no matter how the Antichrist has organized his evil plan against Christ, that Christ will still defeat him with ease. No matter how skilled the kings of the earth will be, this will be one war that their armies will have no chance of winning; no military intelligence can outwit the great, the powerful, and the omniscient King of Kings. We are also told that the beast and the false prophet were cast into the lake of fire alive, which burns with brimstones. It's interesting that the Antichrist, as well as the false prophet, will be thrown into the lake of fire before Satan. The remnants that were left over were slain with the sword of him that rode upon the white horse. Christ's sword is his righteous words of judgment that will proceed from his mouth. The apostle Paul said in regards to this event that "And then shall that Wicked be revealed, whom the Lord shall consume with the spirit of his mouth, and shall destroy with the brightness of his coming" (2 Thess. 2:8–9). Again, to show the horrendous judgment of God, the carnivorous birds of the air will dine heartily upon the flesh.

20:1–6

After the Antichrist and his false prophet were thrown into the lake of fire, John saw an angel descending out of heaven with a key to the bottomless pit and a great chain in his hand. The word *key* in this text should be interpreted as given power or permission. It is to be taken figuratively; it is the Greek word κλεις/*kleis*. The bottomless pit is a deep place where evil spirits go to be imprisoned. They also can be let out from time to time. It is the Greek word αβμσσος/*abussos*, meaning *abyss* or "extremely deep place." However, the bottomless pit should not be taken to mean *hell* or "the lake of fire."

The devil will be bound to this abyss for one thousand years by this powerful angel. After the angel cast the devil in the pit for a thousand years, he set a seal upon him, that he should not deceive the nations no more till the thousand years should be fulfilled. After that, he should be loosed for a little season.

Listen, there comes a time when all who claim Christ as Savior will be put to a test. The testing of the believers' faith will motivate him to take personal inventory of their convictions; it will validate if their souls are really secure in Jesus. The apostle Paul said, "Yea, and all that will live godly in Christ shall suffer persecution" (2 Tim 3:12). Jesus also said, "No man, having put his hand to the plough, and looking back, is fit for the Kingdom of God" (Luke 9:62).

After John saw Satan being cast in the bottomless pit, he saw thrones and those who sat upon them. Now when I think of thrones, I think of a position of ruling authority, or one who has been given authority by someone or by a group of people. To assist me with this idea of thought, I think of how we as voting individuals elect judges to sit on that chair or throne of authority to judge legal court matters. Therefore, the people that John saw sitting upon thrones were given authority by God to rule and judge matters during the millennium (Dan. 7:9–10, 22; Matt. 19:28).

Those who will be given this position will be all those who will be part of the first resurrection such as Christ, the Raptured Church, and the tribulation saints as well as the Old Testament saints (Dan. 12:1–2; 1 Thess. 4:16).

The words "They shall be priests of God" should be interpreted as the entire nation of Israel. The nation of Israel is God's people and will always be. He will fulfill his promise that he spoke to his servant Moses. God says to Moses, "And ye shall be unto me a kingdom of priests, and a holy nation. These are the words which thou shalt speak unto the children of Israel" (Exod. 19:6).

20:7–10

When the thousand-millennium period ends, Satan shall be loosed out of the prison of the abyss. He shall go out in his wickedness to deceive the nations throughout the world. The names Gog and Magog are to be taken symbolically to describe earth's last rebellion against Christ. This is when Satan is going to influence some of the rulers of earth to rebel against Christ after the millennium.

We get this train of thought from Ezekiel 38 and 39, when Gog of the land of Magog attacked Israel. In Jewish thought Gog and Magog stood for everything that was and is against God. Therefore, when we look at verse 8, Satan is going to lead an immense number of rebellious leaders along with their people to fight and rebel against Christ. Satan's army will encompass the city of Jerusalem. However, the strength of their number will be no match for the all-powerful Christ. Their demise will be quick and effective. God will utterly destroy them by bringing down fire from heaven to devour them. However, this will not be his final end; his final and everlasting judgment will take place when God casts him in the lake of fire to be punished eternally.

20:11–15

After John witnessed Satan being cast into hell, brought on by Christ's judgment, he saw a Great White Throne and God sitting upon it. The whiteness of the throne depicts God in the pureness of his judging. He could not be bribed, nor could he be influenced to look the other way. His judgment is true and righteous. The Psalmist said, "Clouds and darkness round about him: righteousness and judgment are the habitation of his throne" (Ps. 97:2).

When John spoke and said that the earth and heaven fled and that there was no place found for them, he was saying the God was finished with the old heaven and earth (see Ps. 114:7, 8; 2 Pe. 3:7, 10–12). The former things are passed away.

The unsaved, many of whom were standing before God's throne, were judged from out of two books: the book of life and another book, which is the book of deeds. Daniel said, "The court sat in judgment, and the books were open" (Dan. 7:10). It goes without saying that God keeps a record of all deeds (v.12).

The second book is the book of life. This is the book that contains all the believers of the righteous. When the lost stand before the Great White Throne of God and find that their name is not written in the book of life, then they will be cast into the lake of fire. No unbeliever will be exempt from this final judgment of doom. Even those who have died by way of the sea will be raised during the second resurrection for judgment. Even those who were cremated and their ashes tossed in the sea for burial will be embodied for judgment.

Death and hell will be cast into the lake of fire. Death, which is the last enemy of man, is personified in the bodily image of a person. The word *hell* or *hades*, which is the word *hell* translated in the New Testament, is the place of the unseen dead. Both will meet its final destination in the lake of fire. Which is also the second death. The second death is for those of the second resurrection—the unsaved, which is eternal separation from God.

21:1-2

In this chapter, John stands as a witness to see the new heaven and the new earth; this is that place that God had prepared for his prepared people. John, as a heavenly guest, gazes as an informative reporter on the things that he saw concerning the eternal state. Notice if you will that John used the word *new* to describe the heaven and the earth that he saw. The Greek word is καινος/*kainos*, meaning qualitatively new.

This is to say that the new heaven and earth was not just a reproduction of the old, but a total look that is different from that which was previously made. The quality will be so good that it could not be imagined by the thoughts of man. The word *heaven* in this verse speaks about the firmament, the sky and solar system, the moon, the stars, etc. It should not be confused with the third heaven where God dwells (1 Kings 8:30; 2 Cor 12:2).

Well, since we are on the subject of the third heaven, what are the first and second heaven? Again, the first heaven could be the atmosphere or sky, including the clouds (Gen. 8:2) The second heaven can mean space, sun, stars, and the solar system (Isa. 13:10). We know that the earth is going to be different, because John said that there will be no more sea. Think about it. When the sea and oceans disappear under the commands of the greatest architect that is God, just think of the space that will be available for God to use at his will. In other words, God is going to make and reshape the old earth to become a new, better-quality earth. The apostle Paul said, "But as it is written, Eye hath not seen, nor ear heard, neither have entered into the hearts of man, the things which God hath prepared for them that love him" (1 Cor 2:9).

The holy city, which is the New Jerusalem, is also a place that fits under the umbrella of 1 Cor 2:9; for mankind cannot even imagine the full beauty and description of what God has made for his people. John sees the New Jerusalem descending from God out of heaven. The city was beautifully arrayed, like a bride that is beautifully prepared and dressed to meet her oncoming husband at the altar.

Now even though the marriage of the Lamb was just before the millennium, that is when Christ received her bride, the Church. The holy city, the New Jerusalem, will not come down beautifully prepared for the believers of Christ until after the millennium, which will be after a thousand years and after Satan gets cast into the lake of fire. The New Jerusalem was not something that God just quickly threw together; it was not something that he just did out of spontaneity. It was a place that he had prepared after his ascension to his Father, that is after his earthly crucifixion. Christ told his disciples, "I go to prepare a place for you. And if I go and prepare a place for you, I will come again, and receive you unto myself; that where I am, there ye may be also" (John 14:2–3).

Listen, followers of Christ, the holy city had no choice but to look good, because it was God that made it and prepared it. Everything that he does is good. Matter of fact, his résumé says in the book of Genesis that everything that he made was good (Gen. 1:31).

As we continue, we see that John heard a great voice from heaven saying, "Behold, the tabernacle of God is with men." The voice that John heard was probably the same angel in Revelation 19:5 who was noted of making a heavenly announcement for all to praise God because the marriage of the lamb was about to take place (Rev. 19:5–8).

This same angel, no doubt with his great and mighty voice, was now making an announcement about the New Jerusalem. He said loudly for all to hear that "the tabernacle of God is with men and he will dwell with them and they shall be his people and God himself shall be with them, and be their God." What does this announcement mean? To explain this, let's look at the word tabernacle in the Greek Language. It is the word σκηνη/*skene*, meaning *tabernacle* or *tent*.

When Israel was being led through the wilderness by Moses, God gave instruction to him to make or build him a sanctuary/tent, so that he may dwell among them (Exod. 25: 8–9). To show God's presence within the tent he chose and illuminated a cloud descending upon it. This was known as his shekinah glory. When Solomon's temple was being dedicated, the shekinah glory of the Lord filled the temple like it did when the glory cloud descended upon the tent in the wilderness (1 Kings 8:10, 11).

However, the descending cloud upon the tent and upon Solomon's temple was symbolic of the presence of God, like a portable tent that is set up and taken down. It would come and then it would go. However, when the angel announced loudly that the tabernacle of the Lord was with men, it was to show the permanent presence of God and not a temporary presence. God would finally dwell with his people forever.

Also, within the third verse, the angel is declaring that the people of God are actually God's people. And as God's people, they will dwell eternally with God forever (cf. Lev. 26:11–12; Jer 31:33; Ezek. 37:27).

The angel also said that God himself will wipe all tears from their eyes. Living with God in eternity will be of great joy and jubilation. The tears of sorrow will be no more; pain, grief, and death will cease to exist anymore.

He that sits on the throne is no other than God himself; he says that he makes all things new. Again, it's that Greek word καινος/*kainos*, meaning "new in quality," "recently made," *fresh*.

God will bring in a new creation for the creatures that are in him (2 Cor 5:17). The old things, along with the old creation, will no longer exist. The prophet Isaiah said, "Remember not the former things, nor consider the things of old. Behold, I am doing a new thing" (Isa. 43:18–19).

It is God who says that he will make all things. No one has that ability to create but God. The angel affirms and agrees with what God had said and tells John to write it down because it is coming from the one who is faithful and true. When God says things, one must believe it; he cannot lie. His word and presence have been around before the foundation of the world. God says to John that He is alpha and omega, the beginning and the end. Christ then tells John that he will satisfy all who desire and thirst after him. He will be unto them a fountain of living waters.

The waters of his presence and teachings will be free to all. Jesus said, "Blessed are they which do hunger and thirst after righteousness: for they shall be filled" (Matt. 5:6). Because of their overcoming faith, the believers will inherit the things of God. John said in 1 John 5:4, "For whatsoever is born of God overcometh the world: and this is the victory that overcometh the world, even our faith."

Contrary to the benefits of the believers, those who have not a genuine relationship with Christ will be sentenced to hell, which is the lake of fire. The unbelievers consist of the following: the fearful, the Greek word δειλος/*deilos*, meaning *timid*, or "to be fainthearted," or *cowardly*.

The fearful are those who refused to take a stand for Christ when it was necessary. The fearful are those who were ashamed to mention the name of Christ, because of oncoming retaliation and consequences that will surely come to them (see Mark 8:38; Luke 9:26; Roman 1:16). The unbelieving are those who have not a personal relationship with Christ. The Greek word is *απιστος/apistos*, meaning "without faith," *faithless*, "not to be trusted," "without trust in God," and "one who disbelieves in Christ" (see John 3:18).

The abominable are those who don't care how they live their lives before God; they are those who have polluted their lives by living immoral and wicked lives, and because of this, they are distressed before the eyes of the Lord. The Greek word is *βδελυσσω/bdelusso*, and it means "to render foul," "to abhor," "metaphorically to abhor," or "to detest." (Lev. 18:30; Proverbs 8:7).

The murderers will also share their eternal damnation. To understand the full scope of their murderous lifestyle, there are three words in Greek that define wicked and immoral actions.

First, it is the word *φονευς/phoneus*, which means to "commit a homicide or kill." Second, it is the word *ανθροποκτονος/anthropoktonos*, which means "to be killed" "or put to death" or *manslayer*.

Third, it is the word *σικαριος/sikarios*, which means to be an assassin or a murderer (Exodus 20:13; Num 35:17–18). In other words, those individuals who have a lifestyle of being a murderer, or have hired assassins to kill, will have hell as their reward.

As we continue with the list, we come to the word *whoremonger*. It is the Greek word *πορνος/pornos*, which means "to sell," a male prostitute or fornicator; the Greeks considered one who prostituted himself for gain as *pornos* (Eph 5:5; 1 Cor 6:9; 1 Tim 1:9–10).

Next on the list of the lifestyle of the lost are sorcerers. What exactly are sorcerers? *Webster's Dictionary* defines the word as "a person who practices: a wizard or warlock; a person who used his power for evil ends." The Greek word is *φαρμακευς/pharmakeus*, and it means "to administer a drug," "an enchanter with drugs," and "a magician." Sorcery is a practice that is forbidden by God.

Those who take part in such a craft put their faith in the dark arts (Satan), rather than putting their faith in the one true God (Jehovah). Moses tells the children of Israel, "There shall not be found among you any one that maketh his son or his daughter to pass through the fire, or that useth divination, or an observer, or witch, or a charmer, or a consulter with familiar spirits, or a wizard, or a necromancer. For all that do these things are an abomination unto the Lord: and because of these abominations the Lord thy God doth drive them out before thee. Thou shalt be perfect with the Lord thy God. For these nations, which thou shalt possess, hearkened unto observers of times, and unto diviners: but as for thee, the Lord thy God hath not suffered thee so to do" (Deut 18:10–14; see also, cf. Psalm 58:5; Acts 13:6–12).

The next lifestyle of the unbelievers that is mentioned are idolaters. Paul tells the Church of Corinth that "Know ye not that the unrighteous shall not inherit the Kingdom of God? Be not deceived, neither fornicators, nor idolaters, nor adulterers, nor effeminate, nor abusers of themselves with mankind" (1 Cor 6:9; cf. 1 Cor 5:11; Eph 5:5; Rev. 22:15).

The Greek word is ειδωλολατρης/*eidololatres*, and it means "a worshipper of false gods," "a servant or worshipper of an idol." Moses tells Israel, "Thou shalt have no other gods before me. Thou shalt not make unto thee any graven image, or any likeness of anything that is in heaven above, or that is in the earth beneath, or that is in the water under the earth. Thou shalt not bow down thyself to them, nor serve them: for I the Lord thy God am a jealous God" (Exod. 20: 3–5b).

The next lifestyles to be judged are all liars. The Greek word is ψευδης/*pseudes*, which means *lying*, *deceitful*, *false*, and *untruth* (cf. Exod. 20:16; Prov. 8:7; 1 Tim. 1:10). We are told that the doom and the judgment of those who live contrary to the life of Christ will have their part in the lake of fire, which is the second death, which burns with fire and brimstone. This second death is total separation from God; it's a literal hell of everlasting torment of fiery suffering.

John now changes his subject from describing the doomful state of the wicked to hearing a voice of one of the seven angels, which had the seven vials full of the last plagues. The angel invited him to come with him, and in doing so, he will be shown the Lamb's wife. There are two views concerning the identity of the lamb's wife or bride. First, some say that the identity of the wife is the holy city—the New Jerusalem.

They say this because this is what is being said in this verse (10). In that verse it says, "And he carried me away in the spirit to a great and high mountain, and showed me that great city, the holy Jerusalem, descending out of heaven from God." Some believe like I do that the bride of Christ is the Church.

We get that understanding from Revelation 19:7–8, which states, "Let us be glad and rejoice, and give honor to him: for the marriage of the lamb is come, and his wife hath made herself ready. And to her was granted that she should be arrayed in fine linen, clean and white: for the fine linen is the righteousness of the saints." So how can we explain this, since both can be supported by scripture? Revelation 19:7–8 is referring to believers, saints, and the righteous, which makes up the universal church. In other words, it consists of all believers from the day of Pentecost to the Rapture of the Church. Revelation 21:2, 9, and 10 speaks more and describes a city.

This is what I propose: the marriage of the Lamb to the Church happens after the Rapture and before the millennium. The New Jerusalem, as the wife of Christ/Lamb, takes place during the eternal state. Therefore, the city that John saw was a city filled with the Church, or believers of Christ, even though the description is of the city itself.

The holy city will depict the glory of God. Its light is compared to the illustrious glimmer of precious stones. Stones such as jasper and crystals. The city is an illuminous city of great light. The Greek word for *light* in this verse is the word φωστηρ/*phoster*, meaning *brilliant light*, or *source of light*. Since Christ will be in the city, his glory will be the giver of the light of the city. Jesus said, I am the light of the world (John 9:5).

He will also be the light of the New Jerusalem. John the revelator said, "The city doesn't need any sun or moon to give light, because the glory of God gave it light, and the lamb was its lamp" (Rev. 21:23).

The city had a great high wall, and on each side there were three gates: three in the east, three in the west, three in the south, and three in the north. Written upon each of the gates was the name of one tribe of Israel. There were also twelve angels. Gates represent going and coming. Believers will be able to come as they please into the New Jerusalem.

The city will also have twelve foundation stones with the names of the twelve written upon them. The Greek word for *foundation* is the word θεμελιος/*themelios*, meaning metaphorical doctrine or to give instruction, or foundation of truth. It was the apostles of Jesus that laid the foundation of the Church (Acts 1:1–2; Eph 2:20).

21:15-20

As we move on, we see that John saw the angel measure the New Jerusalem with a golden reed, simply a measuring stick or rod. This was not the first time that measuring rods were used as a form of measurement. In Ezekiel chapter 40 to 45, Ezekiel saw within a vision a man using a measuring rod to measure the temple in millennium kingdom, as well of the holy city. In these verses, John saw an angel measuring the holy city.

Notice the color of the measuring rod. It was gold to depict the quality and value of the city. The city measured 12,000 furlongs on every side. A furlong is equivalent to 600 feet. Therefore, the city was in the shape of a cube, which included the length, width, and height measured 1500 miles on each side. The walls of the city measured 144 cubits. The measurement of a cubit is about 21 inches, and it's usually the length of a man's elbow to the tip of his middle finger. Therefore, the walls stood about 216 feet. The city itself was of pure gold; it shone like transparent glass.

The structured walls of the city were transparent as jasper stones. Jasper in Greek is ιασπις/*iaspis*, meaning "a stone with various colors like purple and green." The foundations of the city walls were the colors of every precious gems, such as jasper (clear like a diamond), sapphire (blue in color), chalecedony (greenish in color), emeralds (green in color) sardonyx (red in color), sardius (fiery red), chrysolyte (golden yellow), beryl (color is green), topaz (greenish yellow), chrysoprasus (goldish green), jacinth (color of violet), and amethyst (it's color is purple).

These twelve stones made up the twelve foundations of the city and also had the names of the twelve apostles upon them.

21:21-27

The city itself has twelve gates made of pearls, four gates on each side. The streets of the city are translucent; it is also pure gold. Again, gold depicts the glory of God. It also depicts the city as having enduring beauty and quality. John also said that he noticed that there was no temple within the holy city. Why? You may ask. Well, because God the Father and Christ the Lamb is the temple.

Earthly structures such as church buildings remind us of the place where God dwells. The tabernacle in the wilderness, the Ark of the Covenant, reminds us of the place where God dwells. The body as the temple of the Holy Spirit reminds us of the presence of God. But in the New Jerusalem, God is the temple. His presence, his divine glory, will give light to the holy city as we worship him throughout eternity.

There will be no need of sunlight, no need of moonlight, because the glory of the Lord will light the city. The prophet Isaiah said, "The sun shall be no more thy light by day; neither for brightness shall the moon give light unto thee an everlasting light, and thy God thy glory. Thy sun shall no more go down; neither shall thy moon withdraw itself: for the Lord shall be thine everlasting light, and the days of thy mourning shall be ended" (Isa. 60:19-20).

Verse 24 speaks of a time when all of God's people will come to him in the eternal state and worship him in the New Jerusalem. People from all nations, as well as their kings, will be a part of this great universal worship.

The Church will be there, God's chosen people—the Jews will be there (cf. Isa. 2:2-4; 11:12; 54:5; 56:6-8); all who enter will enjoy the presence of God's light.

"The day will come when the Lord will be king over all the earth; in that day there will be one Lord" (Zachariah 14:9).

They will come unified and with one purpose, and that is to honor, worship, and praise the King of Kings. The city will be open to all who love the Lord; it will never close. The darkness of night will no longer be prime time for crime. For dread of night, as an opportunity to sin, will no longer exist; for night and the former things will pass away.

No crime will be in the city; they would have already been cast into the lake of fire. Not one person from any nation will bring defilement or abominations into the city. Therefore, only the righteous and the pure in heart shall worship God in the holy city. Only those whose names are written in the Lamb's book of life will get the opportunity to worship God in spirit and in truth.

They will come to give God tribute and glory forevermore. Yes. They will come to worship him in the beauty of his holiness, while at the same time those at the gates of the city will open their hands to receive them eternally.

22:1–5

As I attempted to comment on the last chapter of the book of Revelation, my heart became overwhelmed with joy as I read on how God will eternally feed and heal his people forever. The angel showed John a pure and clear river flowing from the throne of God; the river is known as the river of life. When Christ reigns on earth, he will tell his followers that he came to give life and to give it more abundantly (John 10:10).

When he spoke to the Samaritan woman at the well, he says to her that whoever drinks from this earthly well will thirst again, but whosoever drinks from the well that he is able to give will never thirst (John 4:13–14).

But now we see the promise of this fulfillment even in heaven. Therefore, not only is Christ the fulfillment of living water on earth, but he is also the source of the living water in heaven. Yes. Christ is the source of the water of life. In the middle of the street, and alongside the river, stood the tree of life. The tree produces twelve kinds of fruits, each month a different type of fruit. It is therefore a fruit tree.

The leaves of the tree were for the healing of the nations. Verse 3 informs us that the New Jerusalem will not be affected by the old curse that God pronounced upon the old earth (see Gen. 3:14–19; Zech. 14:11; Mal 4:6).

In other words, no longer will there be a cause and effect of sin. Sin will no longer exist. God and his son will be the presence in the city, and their presence will motivate their people to serve them. The Greek word for *serve* is the word λατρευω/*latreuo*, and it means "to serve in a religious sense" or "to worship." God's followers shall see his face, and his names shall be in their foreheads.

As true worshipers, the eternal state believers will be allowed to behold the face of God. What a privileged joy that will be, when we get to see God face-to-face! If you can remember, the scripture tells us that "no man hath seen God at any time, the only begotten Son, which is in the bosom of the Father, he hath declared him" (John 1:18).

However, when we worship God in the New Jerusalem, we will see him face-to-face! Yes. We will behold him and worship him forever. Again, to validate seeing God, as we worship him in the New Jerusalem, Jesus promised us, "blessed are the pure in heart: for they shall see God" (Matt. 5:8).

Each individual worshipper will bear the name of God in their forehead. This is to mean that we will belong to God and that we are his eternal representatives. Also, within the vision that John saw of the holy city was that night was no more, because God gave light to the city.

In other words, as worship goes up to God by his people forever, God's divine brilliance and glory will light up the city forever.

22:6–9

To show the importance of what the angel was showing John, he tells him that what he had just shown him was true and faithful, and it was of God's holy will for him to share this important message to John. It was a message of urgency because Christ could come at any moment.

The Greek word for *quickly* in verse seven is the word ταχύ/*tachu*, meaning *rapidly*, *swift*, or *promptly*. It behooves all to be mindful of the importance of accepting Christ as Lord and Savior. Time is running out! The Church will be Raptured, the bema judgment will take place, the marriage of the Lamb will take place, the tribulation period will happen, the millennium period will occur, and the Great White Throne and the eternal state will take over for certain.

Therefore, one must know without a shadow of a doubt that their soul is secured in the Lord. Christ's words, "Behold, I come quickly" should be words that captivate the hearts of many and make them ready themselves for Christ. Also, this verse lets us know that when we keep and live the blessed saying of this prophecy, we will be blessed as well.

After John saw and heard of the things that the angel revealed unto him, he fell down at the angel's feet. However, the angel, knowing that the only one who is worthy of worship is God. He told John to get up because he was just a servant just like he is.

This response by the angel should remind us that only God should be worshipped. No matter how gifted or charismatic a person may be, all glory and worship should be directed toward God. The response of the angels also demonstrated the humility of the angel. Man ought to live a life of humility and not like Satan, who wanted to ascend into heaven and who wanted to exalt his throne above the stars and be like the most high (Isaiah 14:12–15).

It reminds me when Peter, James, and John beheld the transfiguration of Christ, and Peter said, "Let us build three tabernacles: one for Moses, one for Elijah, and one for Christ." God immediately spoke up and said, "This is my beloved son, in whom I am well pleased; hear ye him" (Matthew 17:1–8).

22:10–16

John was told not to seal up the sayings of the prophecy. Why? Because the time had come for all to realize that the time of believing in Christ, as Lord and Savior, was now. The time had come for all to open their hearts to Christ, as they read about him in the book of his prophecy. The apostle Paul said on one occasion that "now is the acceptable time unto salvation" (2 Cor 6:2). When Daniel was given instructions to "seal up the vision, for it pertains to many days hence" (Dan. 8:26).

The instructions given to Daniel were to show that many things have to take place before God reveals his plans concerning apocalyptic events. But now it was a time to read what was seen and spoken. Why? Again, the coming of Christ could take place at any moment.

It was time for all men to consider their ways, repent, and accept the Lord Jesus as their King. Or they can get left behind and go through the tribulation period or, even worse, be cast in hell, where the devil and false prophet will be.

But nevertheless, people will still not heed the warning; they will continue to live an unrighteous lifestyle. The words "He that is unjust, let him be unjust still: and he which is filthy, let him be filthy still" informs us that there are going to be a lot of people who refuse the instructions that are written in this book; they will continue to live an unholy life. However, there are going to be many who will take heed of these instructions and will continue to live a righteous life in Christ.

The words "and he that is righteous, let him be righteous still: and he that is holy, let him be holy still" confirms the faithful walk of the true believers. Despite trials and tribulations, the faithful in Christ will continue to live faithful, no matter what opposition comes their way. Christ tells the Church of Ephesus, "Be thou faithful unto death, and I will give thee a crown of life" (Rev. 2:10).

In other words, Christ encourages, as well as informs, the righteous to keep on living a victorious life of faith because the day will come when they will be rewarded with eternal life; they will eternally worship with Christ in the eternal state forever. When Christ returns, he said that he will be bringing rewards with him.

The Greek word for *reward* is the word μισθός/*misthós*, meaning either *wages* or *reward*. This is to say that when Christ returns, he will give mankind their just wages that is due to them. Some will be given rewards based on their works of righteousness and others based on their works of unrighteousness.

Everyone will receive their just desserts; it will be based upon their deeds done in their body, rather they be good or bad. Again, these deeds will reflect their relationship that they have with Christ. If their deeds reflect their faithfulness in Christ, then they will be rewarded. If their deeds imply that they are unrighteous, then they will not be accepted into God's kingdom. Why? Because faith without works is dead. Why? Because their lifestyles were not a result of them accepting Christ as Lord, and their works sealed their fate. (cf. 2 Cor 11:15; Rev. 20:13).

Christ validates the authenticity of this prophecy by saying that he is the alpha and the omega, the beginning and the end, the first and the last. He says this to remind all that his deity is everlasting. No mortal man can make such a statement. It is Christ that has been existing, even before man put a date on a calendar.

The Lord Christ is eternal. He is the beginning. And yes, he is the end. Matter of fact, he said these words in the beginning of the book of Revelation, and now he says them at the end (1:8, 17; 2:8). Christ is eternal and sovereign, and because he is God, he always finishes and fulfills what he sets out to accomplish. He is the author and finisher of our faith (Hebrews 12:1–2).

As we look at verse 15, we are informed about the eternal relationship that believers have in Christ. First, we are told that they are blessed. The Greek word for *blessed* is the word $\mu\alpha\kappa\alpha\rho\iota\circ\varsigma$/*makarios*, meaning "possessing the favor of God," *blessed*, or "to be happy." This is to say that the life of the believer is one that is blessed. Blessed because their joy and happiness is the result of having a genuine relationship with Christ; they also have the favor of God upon them because they practice and live God's commandments. Jesus said, "If ye know these things, happy are ye if you do them" (John 13:17).

Also, because of the believers' faith in Christ, they will eat the fruit of the tree of life forever. They will have free access into the New Jerusalem as well. However, those who have rejected Christ as their personal Savior and have lived a lifestyle of a sorcerer, whoremonger, murderer, idolater, and liar will not be allowed into the city of God.

By Jesus telling John that he is the one who sent this message to the churches by way of his angel is to prove that Jesus is the authoritative source behind this prophetic book.

Jesus says that he is the root and offspring of David is to say that he is the fulfillment of the prophecy that Isaiah prophesied about in Isaiah 11:1.

22:17-21

As we come to the final verses of this chapter and prophetic book, Christ, as the loving God and Savior, extends a call to salvation. This invitation to be saved is a loving and passionate call to accept him by faith. It's a call that is free to all and is so powerful that it is able to set people free from their sins. The divine source that is used to draw and convict people of their wrongdoing is the Holy Spirit. The Holy Spirit bears witness of the truth (John 14:26; 15:26; 16:7:15).

The bride of Christ is the Church. Therefore, Christ, who is utilizing the work of the Holy Spirit, as well as the Church, is making one last call for all to accept him as Lord. When they accept Christ by faith, they will live with him forever.

The Church are all those who have shared in the decision-making of accepting Christ as Savior. Therefore, it is with great urgency and passion that the Church extends this call to all who are in need of Christ's saving grace; that way, the lost can experience the same saving jubilation that the Church received when they accepted Christ as their Lord and Savior.

Also, Christ used the word Church to demonstrate the purpose of the church as an outreach vehicle to build up the kingdom of God. He did this by utilizing evangelistic ministries to reach others and to bring them into the saving knowledge of Christ (Acts 1:8). In other words, if one's soul is thirsty for completeness and satisfaction, one can get satisfied by drinking the water of life freely and without price. I have discovered over the length of my forty-year ministry that a lot of people live their lives in a state of emptiness. They are always searching for that right thing to fill the void in their souls, but unless they accept Christ as Lord and Savior, they will never be spiritually complete on the inside.

Jesus said, "I am the bread of life: he that cometh to me shall never hunger; and he that believeth on me shall never thirst" (John 6:35). Jesus also said, "If any man thirst, let him come unto me and drink" (John 7:37b; see also John 4:10).

Jesus also adds a warning to those who may add or take away anything from the truth of this prophecy. God's Word is true, and therefore one should not attempt to change the meaning of it. It is the only source that sets men free (John 8:32).

If one does choose to add or change the validity of this book, then they will also add the plagues of this book to their lives as well. Christ closes the prophecy of this book, by once again telling all that he could come at any time.

The lost should seek his salvation, and the Church should stay encouraged knowing that our Lord Christ is coming back with rewards for his faithful. "Surely," Christ says, "I come quickly." The Greek word for *surely* is the word *vaι/nai*, meaning *yes*, *certainly*, *truly*, and *assuredly*. Therefore, it is of a truth that Christ is coming back; his returning is inevitable. There is nothing that anyone could do to stop him. He will truly come back for his Church and to defeat Satan and all his evil works. Hallelujah. The King is coming! Hallelujah, we win!

ABOUT THE AUTHOR

Isiah King has been in the gospel ministry of Jesus Christ since 1979. He is a Pastor Emeritus. He has been married to the love of his life (Nadine) for over thirty-four years. He has three children and nine grandchildren. He was raised in a Christian home by both parents who loved the Lord Jesus. He knew in high school at the age of sixteen that God had called him into ministry. With a hunger to equip himself for ministry, he enrolled at the American Baptist College. He graduated with an associate's degree. He then enrolled at the Moody Bible Institute and received a bachelor's degree in biblical studies. While the momentum wheel of education was yet turning, Isiah pursued a master's degree in ministry at Moody Theological Seminary and attained it with great joy. He has a passion for teaching, preaching and mentoring others for kingdom work. Also, He enjoys fishing!